One Angel

and

Twenty-One Miracles

Eileen Wilcox

One Angel

And

Twenty-One Miracles

An Incredible Journey of Courage and Faith

EILEEN V. WILCOX

Dedication

To my husband, Terry,
and to our five daughters
who all served Julene with unceasing diligence;
and to our neighbors who cared for us
with love for such a long time.

CONTENTS

BOOK III: THE IMPACT OF ONE ANGEL

JULENE WILCOX'S MEDICAL TIMELINE

October 14, 1997: prescribed Amoxicillin for a sore throat

October 15 & 16, 1997: visits to the Utah Valley Regional Medical Center Emergency Room

October 17, 1997: admitted to Utah Valley

October 18, 1997: Life Flighted to the University of Utah Burn Center

October 18, 1997 – April 19, 1998: patient at U of U Burn Center

April 9, 1998 – June 12, 1998: patient at Salt Lake Regional Medical Center Rehabilitation Unit

June 12, 1998 – August 30, 1998: home

August 30, 1998 – September 6, 1998: patient at Eastern Idaho Regional Medical Center

Sept 6, 1998 – November 10, 1998: patient at LDS Hospital

November 10, 1998 – April 25, 2000: home, with periodic trips to LDS Hospital

PROLOGUE

Julene had such a zest for life—and so much enthusiasm for doing even ordinary things. The summer of 1997, when she was twenty-years old, was the happiest time of her life. In almost every aspect of her life, her fondest dreams were coming true. She had wonderful performing opportunities singing and playing banjo in Bluegrass bands, both in Rexburg, Idaho and on tour in Europe. She had many friends and made more everywhere she went. But best of all, she was in love!

Julene returned home at the end of August from her tour in Europe with the Brigham Young University Folk Ensemble. She then left for BYU to be roommates with her sister, Margo, who was her best friend. Things continued to look up for her. Her music auditions went well. She was accepted into the top choir and was selected to be in the university's opera. She was busy and happy in her classes. And to put the icing on the cake, on October 4, her true love, Scott, asked Julene to marry him!

Yet on October 18, 1997, Julene was flown from Provo to the University of Utah Burn Center in Salt Lake City to be treated for a rare and toxic reaction to penicillin. She was put on a ventilator and placed in an induced coma. In this condition, which is often fatal, Julene battled for her life with extraordinary courage and incredible persistence. She was the recipient of miracles—almost on a daily basis. She truly came to know our Lord and Savior, Jesus Christ.

BOOK I

ONE ANGEL

CHAPTER ONE
AN ANGEL IN OUR MIDST

I'm not sure when Julene was first told, "You look just like an angel!" But I know she was not too happy about it when a boy, vying for her attention, said that to her after a choir concert at Ricks College. But it happened other times as well. One time was sincere and was appreciated, as it came from the sister of her fiancé, Scott. Scott's family had attended a performance of the Brigham Young University Folk Ensemble in the Bay area of California. Scott's sister later told me, recalling this performance: "Julene looked just like an angel." Unfortunately, Julene was already in an induced coma when she told me this and was not able to hear those beautiful words.

Angels are blonde

Well, for starters, angels are often depicted as having blonde hair—sometimes gold or even white. Julene, as a baby, had such blonde hair that some called her a towhead. Because my husband and I both have dark hair, many people jokingly asked: "Where did you get such a blonde child—from the mailman?"

Angels typically sing

Julene began to sing at an early age. By the time she was about two years old, she could match pitches and sing little songs. Before she was three years old, she could sing the songs her older sisters were singing. In her first performance at age three-and-a-half, she sang louder than both of her older sisters.

And Julene continued to sing! She wanted to be in choir rather than orchestra. She wanted to take voice lessons. She was in Bel Cantos—the select choir at Madison High School in Rexburg, Idaho. She participated in musicals both in high school and in the community. Her love of the stage and singing came together as she sang and played banjo

3

as part of several Bluegrass bands. At first it was our family Bluegrass band and then the folk ensembles at both Ricks College and Brigham Young University. She sometimes sang for audiences of thousands while on folk dance tours.

Angels are beautiful

I often heard: "Julene is SO BEAUTIFUL!" That was followed by: "Well, all your girls are beautiful." And it was true— her sisters were equally beautiful, but Julene seemed to have a sparkle that caught one's attention.

So Julene was our ANGEL!

Others recognized Julene as an "angel" even when her hair was no longer blonde, her voice was taken from her, and her outward beauty was marred with scars. As Julene lay in a hospital bed, unable to sing, speak, or even breathe without the aid of a machine, visitors recognized they were in the presence of an angel. Sister Olivia King, a speaker at Julene's funeral, said: "I testify to you that every time I walked into that room, I felt that I was in the presence of angels, and one of the sweetest angels laid in that bed."

CHAPTER TWO
THE BEGINNING

In November of 1971, while I was teaching elementary music in Rexburg, Idaho, two of the principals in the school district decided to line me up with one of the several young men from their LDS ward. They started with Terry Wilcox, an eagle scout and returned missionary, who was home after completing Army basic training. We first met when he knocked on my apartment door in December of 1971. We had a few dates before I went to Portland for Christmas vacation. I returned to Rexburg a few days before school was back in session, anxious to get to know Terry better. We saw each other often until mid-January when he left for Provo, Utah, to start school at Brigham Young University. He came home on many weekends, and I went to Utah a few times. When we toured the Provo Temple during the open house, a tour guide winked at us and invited us to "Come back soon!" We did "come back" to a temple, but it was the Idaho Falls Temple where we were married in June 1972.

During the rest of that summer, Terry worked with his dad and brothers on the farm. In the fall we went to BYU together, where he completed his degree in Range Science and I worked on my Master's Degree in Music Education. We had our first daughter, SaraLyn, while in Provo. Although Terry had planned to work for the U.S. Forest Service after graduation, he decided to return to Rexburg and work with his family on the farm. We were living in an apartment in Rexburg when our second daughter, Margo, was born in 1975.

We bought our first house and moved into it in early January, 1976. We were getting nicely settled when the Teton Dam broke on June 6, 1976, and our house was in the path of destruction. The day the dam broke, Terry was farming west of Blackfoot. I loaded our two daughters and a few things into the car and drove to Terry's parents' house in Burton, seven miles west of Rexburg. Terry's dad, Keith said: "Let's go get Eileen's grand piano." So Terry's brothers, Lynn and Ron, his mother, Afton, and I got into a pick-up and drove back to our house. Upon arriving, the guys turned my antique grand piano on its side, breaking a leg off, and rolled it out to the pick-up. My mother-in-law, Afton, wisely placed many of our belongings on the bed or put them up high on shelves, thus saving many of our personal items, such as Terry's gun collection and my 33 LP records. We drove back to their house in Burton only to learn that we needed to evacuate that area as well. When we saw the wall of water coming toward us, we drove south, heading for Afton's father's house in Rigby. I was pregnant with our third child, and after all of this activity and stress, I began hurting. Fearing premature labor or other problems, Keith, along with a neighbor, gave me a blessing and the pain subsided.

The flood left devastation throughout the lower areas of Rexburg. Our neighborhood was particularly hit hard because it was downstream from a sawmill. The logs wiped out almost every home in our subdivision. Ours was one of the few houses still standing, or even still there, but it was off its foundation.

The summer was full of work, both cleaning up flooded items and just caring for our two young daughters, SaraLyn and Margo. We stayed with Keith and Afton until we could move into a house my parents bought on Cornell Avenue in Rexburg. This house was only a block from Ricks College. It was an ideal place to live because I was offered a part-time teaching position in the Music Department.

Our third daughter, Julene, came home to this house after she was born on October 21, 1976. She weighed 7 lbs. 7 oz. and measured 21 inches long. She had brown hair—I guess the angel in her had not come to the surface yet! Actually, I don't remember when the "angel" began to show through, because Julene was not a particularly happy baby. She had a lot of allergies, and her food did not digest easily. Although born with a little bit of dark hair, she soon lost most of it and looked rather bald compared to her older sisters who, as babies, had tons of long dark hair. But Julene's new hair came in blonde! By the time she was two, she would have been classified as a "towhead."

When Julene was still quite a young baby, her sister, Margo, had a life-threatening blood infection that kept her in the hospital for about a week. During this time Julene had a severe ear infection and was given antibiotics. We came to know our newly arrived pediatrician, Dr. Dan Johnson, very well—even inviting him to dinner. He was single and had not had time to make many friends in the community. Later, he was to play an important role in Julene's life.

We moved to our newly rebuilt house on Angela Drive when Julene was about a year old. She slept in a crib in SaraLyn's room, directly across from our room. As I recall, she woke in the middle of the night most nights, and I would get up and nurse her. One night, Julene was crying and I asked Terry to take care of her. He dutifully got up and went to her crib. When she saw him, she cried out, "I want Mama!" So I guess she was a mama's girl from an early age.

I do remember that Julene was sometime uncooperative, maybe not as a baby, but as a toddler. She was particularly difficult when we wanted to take her picture. She would not sit properly for a professional photographer—thus, we have her picture completely off-center. She was uncooperative even with her own father; so, Terry took her picture with her lying on the floor.

Growing up, Julene's wardrobe included plenty of hand-me-down clothes from her two older sisters. Since my mother was a talented seamstress, Julene also had some fun look-alike dresses and outfits that were similar, but rarely identical, to those of SaraLyn and Margo. However, because she was the youngest of three, she got to wear the other versions of these clothes as she grew older.

Julene remembered many things from her early childhood. In her seventh-grade autobiography, she wrote about turning two years old:

> *One of my favorite birthdays was when I was two and I got my own bed—and I could hardly climb on it even without the box springs. My favorite stuffed animal was 'Pinky,' a pink teddy bear, medium size, with orange eyes. I got him from my Grandma and Grandpa Wilcox.*

At an early age, Julene had a mind of her own and found clever solutions. Shortly before she was three years old, my friends from college, Brian and Christine Ence, stayed with us for a few days. Julene objected to sharing her bed and bedroom with the little girl in this family. Instead, she asked to stay with my parents for the night. In later years, she would often ask to spend time with these grandparents when she was not happy with situations at home!

Despite being a bit stubborn, Julene was truly a joy—and it was wonderful to have three daughters so close in age. Julene was definitely bright. She learned to talk quite early and was speaking clearly by the time she was two years old. She started singing along with her older sisters—matching pitches long before the experts say children are able to do so!

A fourth daughter, Carla, joined the Wilcox sisters in December 1979. This sister was to become Julene's playmate and special friend, particularly when she was "too little" to play with the older girls.

Although Julene refers to herself as "shy" (and in some respects she  was), things changed after she began singing for others. Her first real performance on stage with a microphone was May 28, 1980. Terry's Aunt Lorna Wilcox invited our girls to entertain at a dinner for Relief Society, an organization for LDS Women. Julene was three-and-a-half-years old, and I was told she sang louder than her older sisters. Dressed as little cowgirls, they sang: "Chisholm Trail," "She'll Be Comin' Round the Mountain," "Go Tell Aunt Rhody" and "Home, Home on the Range."

Julene attended the preschool at Ricks College, and she loved all the fun things they did. She was terribly disappointed that she was unable to go to kindergarten the next year, since her birthday was after the school deadline of October 15. Along with a few other mothers, we formed our own small neighborhood preschool. This gave both learning and socialization for Julene and her friends.

CHAPTER 3
JULENE STARTS SCHOOL

Because Terry needed special training for his position in National Guard, we moved to Woodbridge, Virginia for three months, arriving in January, 1981. Here he was enrolled in an advanced engineering course at Fort Belvoir, Virginia. Since the school deadline in Virginia was December 31, we put Julene in kindergarten. She loved it. From her autobiography: *"I got to go to kindergarten in the middle of the year. The kindergarten was like preschool. We had ice cream sundaes every Friday. We played outside a lot, and I loved my teacher. I read Margo's first-grade books."*

I believe Julene's kindergarten experience was the time she truly became outgoing. Halfway through the school year, the morning kindergarten switched to the afternoon. Perhaps it was for my convenience, but the school did not have Julene switch times. Consequently, as we walked to school, her former classmates were walking home. They all waved and called her by name. She felt very important. She also got to know all the children in her new class—and they must have thought it special to be friends with the new girl from Idaho.

Even as a five-year-old, Julene remembered many of the things we did while we lived in Virginia. In her autobiography, she recounted our trips to Mt. Vernon (George Washington's home), Monticello (Thomas Jefferson's home), and Valley Forge where we witnessed a re-enactment. She mentioned seeing Benjamin Franklin, in a convincing likeness, on the streets of Philadelphia. On our way home from Virginia, we stopped in Nauvoo, and she remembered many of the historic sites there, especially the blacksmith shop.

While in Virginia, all the girls had violin lessons—but we were only there about 12 weeks. After returning home, SaraLyn and Margo continued with violin lessons in Pocatello with Diane Worley, but Julene and Carla had piano lessons with Diane's mother, Elaine Worley.

On December 1, 1984, Julene was baptized a member of The Church of Jesus Christ of Latter Day Saints. She should have been baptized in November, but Terry was out of town. Because she was so anxious to be baptized, she was very unhappy about waiting.

When Julene was between the ages of eight and eleven, she spent a great deal of time playing with her sister, Carla, who was three years younger. They had such great imaginative games. Carla remembered their bike-riding adventures that combined both a sporting activity with their pretend-world: Recently, she wrote this memory:

Riding bikes was always something Julene and I enjoyed. One thing we loved doing was riding our bikes to the church parking lot. We would ride around on the sidewalks—going up and down the handicapped ramps. We also loved to play "house" with the parking stalls. The large corner spot (or really non-spot) was our condo where we lived. We worked at a different stall and went shopping at other parking spots.

Then one day my world fell apart. I discovered from a comment from a schoolmate that my beloved pink, banana-seat bicycle was too small for me. All of the kids my age were riding 10-speeds. For some people riding a bigger bike would be a simple switch. However, I was terrified of being higher off the ground. Not only was I scared of the higher bike, but I was scared to try riding a 10-speed and fail where someone might see me.

Julene, resourceful as she was, had a solution. She said she would teach me to ride her bike in the garage with the door closed so no one could see me. There in the garage over the course of a few weeks, Julene taught me to ride her bike. I can still remember trying to keep my balance while I went round and round, trying not to crash into the wall or fall off. One day, I decided I was ready and opened the garage door and tried riding straight. It was much easier than going in a circle. Having mastered Julene's bike, we went to Dad and asked him about getting me a larger bike. Dad took me to a store where I picked out my own red Schwinn 10-speed. Now, Julene and I could continue our adventures once more!

One of the activities Julene participated in every summer was Suzuki Institute—a week-long music camp for Suzuki students playing a string instrument or piano. Although she was occasionally signed up as a violin student, she much preferred being there as a pianist. Julene owed much of her early musical training to the wonderful teachers she had in the various Suzuki music programs. The ability to play by ear and the emphasis on memorization made it easy to learn guitar and banjo when she got older.

Julene began writing in a journal at six years old when she received one for her birthday. Apparently after the first short entry, she dictated the next section—because it was readable. By the time she was in sixth grade, she wrote many details of her life. She listed her teachers at school, the pieces she learned on the piano, and the boys she liked—or the boys who liked her. Her writing showed a lot of variety. Many of her entries showed her flare for writing. On October 20, 1987, when she was a day short of being eleven years old, she wrote:

Right now in P.E. we're working on skipping, sliding, galloping and grapevine. Sounds fun? Ha! But the neat thing about P.E. is I get to stand by Jason for warm-ups. That makes the boring stuff not seem so dull. To make it less boring, I watch to see how often I can catch Jason staring at me.

At age 12, Julene wrote about herself:

I am kind of shy. I am kind of sensitive. I don't wear make-up. I like boys. My favorite color is blue. I like people that are cute and nice and outgoing. I wish I were like that. I want to be married in the temple. I would like to travel to Europe and Asia. I think it would be fun to be a world tourist. I want to be an actress in movies."

CHAPTER 4
ADVENTURES IN HIGH SCHOOL

As she attended high school, some things about Julene changed. Julene was no longer shy, but always sensitive. She never wore much make-up and always preferred doing things with boys rather than with girls. She became the type of person she admired: *"cute, and nice, and outgoing."*

When Julene was in ninth grade, it was part of the high school. SaraLyn drove, and all four of our daughters went together. They dropped Carla off at the Middle School building, but unfortunately, she was always late. Then the other three girls went to the high school, and they were on time! Julene dropped out of orchestra to be in choir, starting with the all-girls choir her first two years, and then moving to the select choir her last two years. She also started taking debate and drama classes. Although she never had leading parts, she had a lot of fun in these activities.

Tenth grade was a really different experience for Julene. After Christmas in 1991, our family left for Anniston, Alabama, where Terry again had National Guard training. Julene and Margo were enrolled in high school, but Julene immediately hit roadblocks. The choir teacher refused to have her in choir because she would only be there for 12 weeks, and there was something special planned shortly after we were to leave. There was no orchestra. I suggested they sign up for band— Julene could learn to play marimba and percussion instruments, and Margo could play flute parts on violin since she refused to learn to play an upright bass. Band was supposed to be the place that everyone made friends. Julene wrote about her first 2 days in band:

The next class was band—the dreaded class. All the way over there, I remembered thinking how scary it was and how the kids were going to hate us and how we were going to be laughed at because we were in band and couldn't even play band instruments. When we got there, I wasn't too far off. The director sent me back by the xylophones. The other xylophone player was a real nerd. I mean he had greasy hair and skin, thick glasses, looked like he had never

13

taken a shower, and was furiously reading a science fiction novel. He looked up at me, saw me sit down and quickly got back to "The Dragon Slayer Takes Revenge" or whatever it was called. They started playing and my nerdy partner reluctantly put down his book and stood up looking at the music. During the whole rest of the class, not a single soul acknowledged us or spoke to us. It was rather disheartening after having had such a friendly welcome in our other classes that morning.

The class left for lunch and we followed, not quite knowing what would happen. By some method, which I can't remember, we learned that the classes were required to sit together at lunch, at the same table.

The second day went quite nicely, except Margo went home sick. Then came band. This day no one said a word to me, and they still didn't need me to play the xylophone or similar instruments. I wondered if they would ever need another player. I went to lunch by myself and sat there and looked around at my empty table. No one came to sit there. I felt as if I didn't even exist. I looked up and my teacher from another class, Miz. Eaton smiled at me.

I suddenly felt tears burning down my cheeks and my throat choking up. She must have seen that--because as I wiped my tears with the rough napkin and tried to stop them from coming, she excused herself and walked over to her class. Soon a girl had asked me to come and sit with her and her friends.

I suffered through the rest of the day and when Mom came to pick me up after school, another flood of tears ensued. The next day, Margo and I transferred out of band, into Miz. Gardner's study hall. The year continued successfully, and we were able to make friends in all our classes.

Being in the South was a wonderful experience overall. In addition to learning to understand and to speak "Southern" (an American dialect that definitely exists), our family visited many historic sites, rode on a paddle-wheel riverboat in New Orleans, experienced a sunrise on the Gulf of Mexico, and waded in the water at Panama City Beach in a hurricane. We went to Atlanta, Georgia, to visit the zoo, and went another time to do baptisms for the dead at the LDS Atlanta Temple.

But the most life-changing event was our trip to Opryland, in Nashville, Tennessee. Here Julene had her first banjo lesson from a wandering musician who played for the visitors at the amusement park. She had always said she wanted to play banjo, and this confirmed it.

Our family started learning bluegrass music the summer after we returned to Rexburg. Julene's banjo teacher was a member of Loose Ties, a bluegrass band from Driggs, Idaho—near Jackson, Wyoming. He said he had never had a student who learned so quickly.

As a junior in high school, Julene participated in the "Young Woman of the Year Program" (formerly called the Junior Miss Program). This was a really good experience. For her talent number, she played the banjo and sang "Salty Dog Rag." She was in the top ten finalists but did not win any individual award. However, the end result was even better than the scholarship money she might have had— she learned that it was fun to be on stage. From that point on, she truly loved to entertain.

Faithful journal keeping had been one of Julene's goals since

she received her very first journal at age six. However, it was not until her sophomore year when we returned home from Alabama that she wrote meaningful entries. There were two entries worthy of mention. On June 16, 1993 she told about an outing to Jackson, Wyoming, with friends visiting from Alabama. She described how much fun it had been to ride on the Alpine slide with the young man in the family. Then she wrote:

15

We ate lunch at a little tiny café called Billy's Hamburgers. The guys working there kept staring at me and talking to each other. Finally, they came over to me and said I looked like a younger Merle Streep (however you spell that). I'm not exactly sure who she is except I know she's a movie star. I was quite flattered."

For an aspiring actress, Julene must have been elated. However, her writing of just three days later was a bit sobering. She never shared this with us:

> *Tonight, as I said my prayers, I had a horrible premonition that I was going to die tonight in my sleep & I wanted to write it down somewhere just in case it happens. It occurred to me that I have developed so many talents & done so many things that it seems like perhaps my mission has been accomplished—I hope not yet, because I don't feel very strong in my testimony at this point in time. I think I'll read my patriarchal blessing & make sure.*

Julene loved her years in high school! She did well academically, taking honors classes and making the honor roll. But what she liked best was her social life. She had many friends and had dates to the dances, although she did not have a steady boyfriend. One of her favorite activities was attending the school-sponsored ski program. Perhaps the reason she liked it so much was because she was such a flirt. She would ski with six or seven boys and no girls!

One morning during her senior year, Julene announced to me as she left for school that she was on the final ballot for homecoming queen. I said to her, "Don't be disappointed if you lose." Julene, not feeling very confident, did not dress up for the assembly. But afterward, she went to the office phone and called me: "Mom, you'll never believe it—I'm homecoming queen!" How she basked in the attention and loved the whirl of activities associated with that honor!

Julene graduated with high honors from Madison High School in May, 1994. Terry had become a member of the school board, and he awarded Julene her diploma. Her older sister Margo was a bit jealous because when she graduated the previous year, Terry was on a white-water rafting trip on the Colorado through Cataract Canyon and missed her graduation.

CHAPTER 5
COLLEGE AND BLUEGRASS

About a month after high school graduation, Julene and her three sisters left for Europe for a month-long Folk Dance Festival tour. They were part of the six-member bluegrass band that accompanied the Ricks College Folk Dancers. The group of 30 students and 6 leaders went to France and Spain. I was concerned about the cost of this trip and told the girls not to call home unless there was an emergency because calls from Europe were so expensive. When I got a call from Julene only a few days into the tour, I was more than a little surprised and concerned. I was even more shocked when I heard Julene say: "Our whole family is coming home." I was so stunned that I asked Julene to repeat herself. This time I heard: "Our host family made me call home."

They had a wonderful four-week tour, with many life-changing experiences. One memorable incident took place during a non-denominational church service held in a beautiful cathedral. They listened to the other groups perform. Then to their surprise, the festival leader announced: "The American Band will now play." They had not been told to prepare a song for this event. By switching a couple of instruments with other band members, the four sisters were able to play a family favorite, "Ashokan Farewell," the song from the PBS Civil War Series. It was a beautiful ending to the service.

Another fun incident occurred after a street festival and parade. Christine Geddes, one of the Ricks College leaders and their translator, was not with the band when the French guide said: "You need to play now!" The student leader said: "What should we play?" Again the guide said: "Play NOW!" So they played "Foggy Mountain Breakdown," a spirited banjo piece. Soon Sister Geddes caught up with them and said: "No, no, no—you were supposed to be playing the national anthem." They decided that the people of France had never enjoyed the American national anthem as much as they did that night.

Ricks College provided a wonderful setting for Julene's first two years in college. Her first year, she and Margo lived in an apartment with four other girls, including a set of identical twins. They did lots of fun things together. Julene was in choir, and she took both voice lessons and piano lessons. Florence Bowman had been her voice teacher in high school and continued to teach her at Ricks. They had a wonderful relationship. Her piano teacher, Carol Barrus, commented to me that Julene was one of the most talented students she had ever had—even though piano was not her main interest. Another of her professors, Brent Jones, commented on her love of life and learning. In January, 1996, she was officially nominated to receive the All-American Scholar Collegiate Award by the Music Department Chairman, Dr. M. David Chugg.

Julene and Margo were part of the Ricks College Bluegrass Band. This band was invited to perform at several important venues, such as the Mother's Week Concert (a packed concert that welcomed mothers who came to spend a week with their daughters on campus) and the Talent Showcase, which featured several campus organizations. The

Folk Dancers and Bluegrass Band had another European tour, this time to Germany and Hungary. On these tours, they also performed for LDS audiences. On two of the Sunday night meetings, Julene sang a sacred number: "I Know that My Redeemer Liveth" from The Messiah by Handel.

At the end of her sophomore year, Julene was invited to sing a vocal solo at the graduation banquet. Afterward, Elder L. Tom Perry, a member of the Quorum of the Twelve Apostles, came over to our table, complimented her, and shook her hand.

Of course, graduating from Ricks College and going on to Brigham Young University was another great opportunity for Julene. She was accepted as a vocal performance major—which was a "major" accomplishment. She got to be roommates with Margo again, and they both auditioned for the BYU Folk Ensemble. As a transfer student, the first year was a bit difficult because other students were already established as good performers. She wanted to be part of the tour group, but the instructor said he already had a banjo player. However, he did need a vocalist, so he asked Julene to come audition to sing and play guitar. Then he casually asked Julene if she would like to play banjo for him. After hearing her banjo playing, he said: "Never mind! Julene, you'll play banjo, and he (pointing to the other banjo player) will play guitar." Margo was invited to join this group, playing upright bass. They played for "Christmas Around the World," which had three sell-out performances in the Marriott Center. In the spring they went on a performance tour with the Folk Dancers to California.

Our older girls came home for a few weeks in the summer. On June 12, 1997, our family did an hour and a half program for the Ricks College Summer Concert Series. The day before the performance, we were beset with problems. We were told that the concert had been moved from the Barrus Concert Hall, with its amazing acoustics, to the Kirkham Auditorium. This meant several details had to be altered. However, the most alarming problem was the fact that Julene had been terribly ill after having her wisdom teeth extracted. Infection followed the extraction, and she took the prescribed capsules of penicillin. Almost immediately she became very weak and had difficulty swallowing. Her oral surgeon did not think it was serious, so no one realized she was having an allergic reaction to penicillin. The morning of the performance, her voice was merely a whisper. Terry gave her a priesthood blessing, and gradually her voice came back to some extent. But during the program, the miracle happened! She did her solo, "Art Is Calling To Me," which is a spoof on opera, and she hit a high C and D with ease! This program was the most comprehensive and the most fun our family had ever put on. The first part included solos and small ensembles from classical repertoire; the second half showcased our favorite bluegrass numbers. Julene figured out harmonies for the vocals and came up with novel ideas for the instrumentals, such as adding Star Wars themes to Dueling Banjos. The auditorium was almost filled to its capacity of 960 seats, and they were a very enthusiastic audience. Julene left as soon as the performance was over to travel to California with her boyfriend, Scott. From there, she went to Provo to go on tour with the Folk Ensemble.

The BYU Folk Ensemble tour was an especially long—seven weeks! Again, Margo and Julene were able to go together. It included East European countries where they had never toured. President Merrill Bateman, President of BYU, and his wife Marilyn were with them for ten days while they did shows for the LDS Church in Poland, the Czech Republic, Austria, and Switzerland. They ended the tour by participating in the Festival de Confolens in France, which is one of the most celebrated folk-dance festivals in the world. At this festival, there was a band day. She recorded the events of this day in her journal:

We did a half-hour show (just the band) on a street corner where you really couldn't hear us. Then we did an hour-long concert in a chapel. This show was really fun. The acoustics were really good and we FINALLY sounded really good—the sound we have worked for *all year long. We had the opportunity to do our new songs—blues, gospels, the <u>COOL</u> stuff. It was really fun. One of our guides, Phillippe, started calling me: "Star" after this show. He says that one day I'll be famous & he'll be able to say, "I knew her when . . ." I don't think I'll be famous, but he says "You have the voice and the smile.*

When the festival concluded, they boarded a bus at 2:30 AM and drove to Paris. Arriving at 7 AM, they checked into a hotel, ate breakfast, and went to discover the sights of the city. They had an hour and a half at the Musée d'Orsay, the impressionistic museum next to the Louvre. They ate lunch in the Latin Quarter, visited Notre Dame Cathedral and Saint Chapelle. The team met back at the hotel and held an LDS Sacrament Meeting. From Julene's journal: *"After lunch, we went to the Hard Rock Café & bought tee shirts. Then we went to the Eiffel Tower & took the elevator to the top. It was grand! Just really impressive. I really thought it was fun."* (Perhaps it was even more exciting because on their first trip to Paris, they arrived at the Eiffel Tower just at closing time and were unable to go to the top!) They ended their time in Paris when the team took a boat ride down the Seine River.

While on tour, Julene received letters, flowers, and packages from Scott. And even before she returned home from Europe, she received letters from her host families and the dancers from other teams. It amazed us how many friends she made in such a short time.

Our two travelers arrived home on August 19th, totally exhausted. Spending only 10 days in Rexburg, Margo and Julene left for Provo on a Friday. After moving into their apartment and auditioning for choir on Saturday morning, Julene flew to Oakland to meet Scott, who was returning from a trip to Tahiti. The next day they drove back to Utah together. Julene recorded: *We got to Salt Lake City exactly 12 hours later after a night drive together. We spent the entire time talking. That was so nice—because we hadn't seen each other for so long. There was lots to talk about.*

Julene's second year at BYU started out just perfect. She made it into BYU Singers, was cast in the Opera, <u>The Merry Widow</u>, and had a great voice teacher. In her journal, Julene wrote: *"School started on Tuesday, and although it is great to be back in school, it feels really weird, especially after such a wild summer."* She and Scott had a New Testament class and a social dance class together.

Julene's journal entries were sparse in September. She wrote: *It's been quite hard to balance my time between all the things I want to do and all the things I have to do.* " She wrote about a date with Scott when they went disco skating:

> *First we went to Savers—a second-hand store and bought each other some 70's clothes. Scott picked out the sweetest outfit for me to wear. I have a pair of brown bell-bottoms, with an elastic waist—oh, all polyester—I forgot to mention. The shirt is basically brown with orange and white and tan swirly things all over it. Then I had a scarf to tie around my neck. We had so much fun. It's just great to be able to go out and be wild and crazy. I loved it."*

On September 15, 1997, Julene told of a very hectic day, but concluded with:

> *"Tonight, however, was the best! We went to President Bateman's for a Folk-Dance Tour Reunion. It was <u>SO</u> much fun. We had a terrific dinner and watched a few slide shows. It was great fun to swap photos and just to see everyone again. I really enjoyed myself."*

Although too busy to write the details of this day as they happened, Julene wrote on October 11th:

> *So much has happened that the news I have to report today is lacking all the background. Last Saturday (October 4) Scott and I drove up to Conference in Salt Lake. On the way I tried to hint and find out what he was planning to do concerning our marriage. As you . . .*

The entry ends there, unfinished. But there is a picture of the two of them with Salt Lake Temple in the background. That night she called to tell us they were engaged.

Shortly thereafter, they made a reservation to be married in the Oakland LDS Temple on December 20th. We planned to have the wedding reception in Victorian style and have the costumes look like those portrayed in Dicken's "A Christmas Carol." Julene wanted to wear my wedding dress that was heavy white lace and with Juliet-style sleeves and a stand-up collar. Her sisters we would have long, plaid taffeta dresses and a Victorian-style bonnet.

When I started looking into airline reservations, I had the feeling, "Don't make reservations yet!" I didn't think too much about it, only wondering if it might be better to make sure of the exact dates of when we needed to go.

However, on October 12, Julene called to say she was getting sick. Then on October 15, her sister, SaraLyn, called to say that Julene was extremely ill, and that we should come to Utah as soon as possible. Suddenly, in that instant, all of our lives were changed forever.

BOOK II

TWENTY-ONE MIRACLES

CHAPTER SIX
THE BURN CENTER AND MIRACLES ONE THROUGH NINE

When Julene called me on October 12, 1997, and said she was not feeling well, I suggested some herbal remedies that had worked well for our family. Because she had not improved, but had developed chills and a fever, I suggested she go to the University Health Center. I knew Scott was planning to give her a diamond engagement ring the coming weekend, so it seemed imperative that she feel well quickly! The doctor who treated Julene suggested that the results from a throat culture would take three to four days. However, antibiotics would help her immediately. So, on October 14, he prescribed the broad-spectrum antibiotic, amoxicillin. After taking only two capsules, her life was quickly turned upside-down. By midnight, she was so ill that her brother-in-law, Eric, came and gave her a priesthood blessing. He then took her to the Utah Valley Hospital Emergency Room. There, a doctor decided it was mononucleosis, even though the "mono" test was negative. Julene was given a different antibiotic, and then sent home. By noon of the next day, she was even sicker and returned to the Emergency Room where eventually, she was sent home a second time. Too ill to climb the stairs to her apartment, she went to Eric and SaraLyn's house.

After receiving several reports of Julene's condition by phone, Terry and I, along with our two-and-a-half-year-old daughter, Audra, drove to Provo. Upon arrival, we were shocked to see Julene's state. She had a rash all over her face, back, and arms, and it seemed to be spreading quickly and progressing into blisters. She was

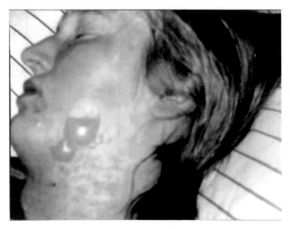

very weak, not able to get out of bed by herself, and at one point she was hallucinating. Not knowing what to do for her, or where to take her when the local hospital hadn't taken care of her, I called Dr. Dan Johnson, her childhood pediatrician, who was practicing in Provo. He ordered some tests from the same hospital. After the tests, we took Julene back to SaraLyn and Eric's house. After Dr. Johnson received the test results by phone, he came directly to their house, took one look at Julene, and immediately called an ambulance. He made sure that capable doctors examined her when she got to the hospital. They weren't sure what was wrong—but she was in very critical condition. Dr. Johnson then called in a dermatologist, Dr. Richard W. Parkinson. He correctly diagnosed it as Toxic Epidermal Necrolysis, a rare and toxic reaction to a drug, in this case to the amoxicillin. Because of the large amount of blistering on her skin (similar to actual burns) and imminent multiple organ failure, she was transported by helicopter to the University of Utah Burn Center, arriving October 18, 1997, at 1:30 a.m.

MIRACLE #1
THE MIRACLE OF MODERN MEDICINE

At the burn center, Dr. Stephen E. Morris explained how serious her condition really was. She was put into a drug-induced coma because the pain was so intense. She was intubated, a procedure where a tube is placed in the mouth that extends into the trachea and is connected to a ventilator and oxygen. Next, they took her into surgery for debridement—or the removal of the injured skin. It was worse than they had expected, and there was damaged and blistered skin over 65-70

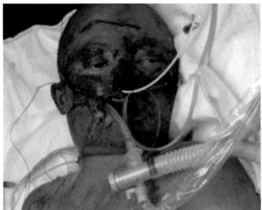

percent of her body. Even her gorgeous hair was shaved off, so they could treat her blistered scalp.

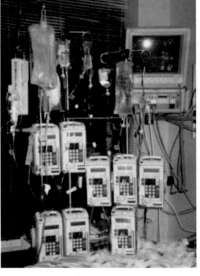

The next morning, we returned to the burn center to find our beautiful Julene wrapped in bandages from head to ankle. Only her feet and one hand still had undamaged skin. We sat with her, even though there was not much we could do except observe while nurses monitored eight I.V. pumps—with tangled tubes everywhere.

The first few days were critical. They explained that infection was a huge danger. Her body was coated with Bacitracin, an antiseptic ointment, and covered with a plastic film that had recently been developed to help save burn patients. The University of Utah Medical School sent photographers to document her condition. [We were given copies, but most are too disturbing to include.] She had to be turned every few hours, and her arms were placed in extensions at night to keep her muscles from tightening.

When Julene's condition did not improve substantially over the next few days, Dr. Morris told us they needed to do a tracheotomy, which is a surgery to insert a tube that goes through a hole made in the throat directly to the trachea rather than through her mouth. Next, they brought in high-tech equipment that cycled her blood through the machine to remove the toxins that were causing the reaction. After this procedure, the reaction began to abate.

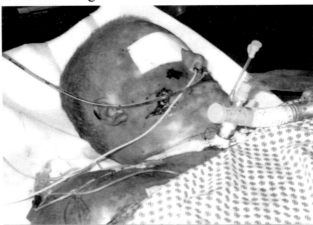

By October 27th, new problems arose. First, her blood pressure dropped. Then a few days later, her oxygen saturation dropped drastically. The doctor decided that it was necessary to open her abdomen to give her more room to breathe. On November 3, they took her to surgery, and left a three-inch wide, eight-inch long gap in her abdominal wall. During this procedure, they discovered how her internal organs and tissues were also badly damaged from this toxic reaction. However, the surgery was successful; and eleven days later, they were able to lower the amount of oxygen she was receiving from 90 to 55 percent, although the actual numbers changed on a daily, or even hourly, basis.

Without any one of these medical procedures—ventilator, oxygen, debridement, plastic film, blood detoxification machine, and further surgery, Julene would not have lived through the first few weeks. We truly experienced the miracle of modern medicine.

"The glory of God is intelligence; in other words, light and truth. All intelligence comes from God, and anyone whose mind is opened to the development of inventions for the benefit and blessing of mankind receives that light and truth through study, through research, through inspiration and guidance from the Spirit of the Lord, whether that individual be a Morse, an Edison, an Alexander Graham Bell, an Orville or Wilbur Wright, or whoever he may be" (Joseph Anderson, "Light and Knowledge to the World," *Ensign,* January, 1973).

MIRACLE #2

THE MIRACLE OF LOVE

Before Julene was put into an unconscious state, Terry, her fiancé Scott, and I told her goodbye and that we loved her. We felt like it would be for a rather short time—days, maybe a couple of weeks; but there were no guarantees. It was frightening in so many ways.

While Julene was in this induced coma, we talked to her, read to her, played beautiful music for her, reassured her that she would get better, and told her that we loved her. We did not know whether in her subconscious state she could hear us, but we realized that loud sounds affected her. One night when Terry and Scott were there, they had a football game playing on her television. Terry remembers that they were talking even louder than the television. Suddenly bells and alarms went off. Nurses came to check on Julene. He said they turned off the television and talked quietly. She settled down, and they decided she had become agitated over the noise and perhaps an unsettling conversation. We were always careful after that to have soothing music and quiet conversations. We wanted to do everything we could to help her recover.

Terry and I were both there during the day for about two weeks, and Scott would come every evening after his classes at BYU. At night he returned to Provo, and we were invited to stay at his grandmother's house in Salt Lake. She welcomed us so very graciously.

Staying by Julene's bedside was not an easy task. There were so many tubes and wires running from machines to her body that Terry called them "spaghetti." There was almost nothing we could do, except watch. One day, Terry called the nurse and asked, "Is this liquid supposed to be dripping all over the floor?" In the array of tubes, one of her medications had not been plugged-in correctly. After that, we felt that we were the extra set of eyes and ears that watched over Julene. Most of the nursing staff appreciated our devotion; some did not.

We were allowed to decorate the wall of the room. Julene's sisters brought a large picture of her—so those who worked with her would know how beautiful she was before this happened. They made decorations,
hung cards from friends, and gave the room a cheery feeling. Looking at Julene's damaged body was so devastating that this bit of  cheer made it much easier to be there with her.

In a burn center, the greatest concern is the need for a sterile environment. Visitors were limited to two at a time, and they had to dress in gowns and hats and were required to scrub carefully before entering. We met with most visitors in the waiting room outside the burn center. This is where we celebrated Julene's 21st birthday—without her presence. Not knowing if she could actually hear us, a few of us were allowed to go into her room and sing to her.

There was a great outpouring of love from her friends, from our friends and neighbors, and from our Rexburg LDS Ward. Her two older sisters, SaraLyn and Margo, came from Provo as often as they could while still keeping up in their classes at BYU.

While Julene may never have heard our words, we know that her spirit was still able to know how much she was loved—and that she was never truly alone.

"A friend loveth at all times" (Proverbs 17:17).

MIRACLE #3
THE MIRACLE OF THE CHURCH OF JESUS CHRIST

When the news of Julene's life-threatening situation became known to our friends, her friends, and many who really didn't even know her, heartfelt prayers were immediately offered in her behalf. Many fasted specifically for a blessing of healing. Her name was put on the prayer roll of several LDS temples throughout the country.

One of those who showed concern was the ward clerk in the Ricks College 10th Ward where Terry was bishop. This young man was a friend of a member of the Quorum of the Seventy, Elder Robert K. Dellenbach. He contacted Elder Dellenbach and asked him to give Julene a blessing.

We received new hope with the visit of Elder Dellenbach. He explained that Terry held the same priesthood that he did, but offered to give her an additional blessing. With Terry assisting, Elder Dellenbach blessed her with healing and recovery. We felt a great peace, as we had faith that his blessing would come to pass.

Elder Dellenbach came to the hospital many times. Sometimes we were there, other times he came late in the evening and would leave a note telling us he had been there. He also shared the story of Julene's struggle with other General Authorities and had her name placed on the First Presidency's Prayer Roll.

When Julene was scheduled for a very critical eye surgery, we invited Elder Dellenbach to give her another blessing. He had had such a busy day that he arrived about two hours after the scheduled time of the surgery. However, there had been delays in the operating room; and miraculously, he arrived about ten minutes before they took Julene to surgery. After the blessing, he turned to me and said: "The day will come when you will thank Julene for her sacrifice for you." I was perplexed by this statement, and my first reaction was: "I will never be thankful for this trial."

Because of the organization of the Church of Jesus Christ, there was a network of Saints who supported Julene, from General Authorities and other General Officers, and especially a member of the Quorum of the Seventy, to members across the United States—maybe across the world. We owed much to those in our midst—our own friends and family as well as to many strangers who prayed in her behalf.

"We believe in the same organization that existed in the Primitive Church, namely, apostles, prophets, pastors, teachers, evangelists, and so forth" (Articles of Faith 1:6)

MIRACLE #4
THE MIRACLE OF THE POWER OF THE PRIESTHOOD

Because Julene's lungs were so damaged, the ventilator forced air into her lungs at quite a high pressure. I was told on Sunday morning, December 7, that she had a pneumothorax—a break or hole in the lung. The air that was forced into her lungs was escaping into the chest area. They made holes under her arms and suctioned the escaped air out of her chest cavity. They explained that this was a life-threatening situation if the lungs did not seal very soon.

Terry was in Rexburg, so I was at the hospital alone. As usual on a Sunday, I went to the LDS Church Service, a sacrament meeting held in the hospital. After the meeting, I asked for the branch president and was told that he wasn't there but would be back in the afternoon. I told the counselor that I needed the branch president to give Julene a blessing.

Later, when the branch president came to her room, I told him what was wrong and asked if he would give her a blessing, sealing her lungs. He gave me a look that showed he felt overwhelmed and said: "I don't know if I can do that." We discussed things for a few minutes, and he promised he would come back later and give her a blessing.

That evening I drove back to Rexburg before the branch president returned. I was very concerned but not distraught, and I felt certain he would bless Julene as he promised he would.

On Monday morning, the doctor from the Burn Center called and told me the result of her morning Chest X-Ray. Her lungs had sealed! Through our faith and that of this devoted branch president, we experienced the miracle available to us through the power of the priesthood.

"Let him ask of God" (James 1:5).
"Therefore ask in faith" (D&C 8:10).

MIRACLE #5
THE MIRACLE OF COMPASSION

While Julene was still unconscious, her body started swelling. This massive water retention problem was a side-effect from her inactivity, from the many drugs she was given, and from her body functioning so poorly. Her head was the size of a basketball—literally. I remember coming into the room to find a nurse-specialist from another hospital making a drainage system to reduce the swelling that was all through Julene's body. There was constantly the need to keep the balance between enough fluid to keep her blood pressure right, and not so much that it caused retention. I remember the lady referring to Julene as "he." I didn't correct her. She looked at Julene's head—swollen larger than one would think possible and looked concerned. Then she noticed Julene's picture on the wall. She turned to me and asked if this was her picture. I nodded, "yes." Her eyes filled with tears, and her face registered pain. [She later heard that Julene was in LDS Hospital and came to visit Julene. She was thrilled to see that she had recovered so significantly from that day she first helped her.]

"Finally, be ye all of one mind, having compassion one of another"
(1 Peter 3:8).

MIRACLE #6
THE MIRACLE OF PEACE

When I left the burn center on Sunday night, December 14, I was quite encouraged. Julene was more stable than she had been thus far. As usual, Terry left Rexburg early Monday morning and stayed with Julene while I taught my classes at Ricks College on Monday and Wednesday. Since Julene's condition improved, Terry came home on Wednesday night instead of waiting until I got to Salt Lake on Thursday. I called to check on her Wednesday night and was told that they had started breathing treatments to thin out the mucus. They used albuterol, a very commonly used bronchodilator. The nurse was excited at how well she was responding to the combination of medicine and suctioning, and how her lungs and bronchial tubes were finally being cleared of the build-up of secretions.

However, on Thursday morning, December 17, we received a call suggesting we both come to Salt Lake. Julene had taken a turn for the worse, and they were concerned she would not survive much longer. Of course, this message put fear in our hearts. We hurriedly gathered a few things and left.

After driving for 30 or 40 minutes, I started pondering what had caused her to change so rapidly. A voice in my mind answered my unspoken question: "It was the medicine they gave her. She will be fine." We drove on to Salt Lake, feeling peaceful and assured that Julene was being watched over. Julene was indeed much better by the time we arrived four hours later. The doctor concluded she had reacted to albuterol and said: "We won't give that to her again!"

"Did I not speak peace to your mind concerning the matter?"

(D&C 6:23)

MIRACLE #7
THE MIRACLE OF RE-AWAKENING

A few days after the incident of treating Julene with albuterol, I recorded in my journal: "Significant improvement—oxygen at 50%." I left for home on Christmas Eve so our family could be together for Christmas. This was the first time in ten weeks that neither Terry nor I had been with Julene for at least part of each day. Our other five daughters had all helped care for each other, as well as supporting us. We needed to have at least this one special day together. Our time together during the holidays was cut short. The day after Christmas we received the call from the burn center telling us they were bringing Julene out of the induced coma.

Julene had been in an unconscious state since October 18. We longed for this day, but feared to find out how much she would remember of all these horrific and painful procedures that had occurred. And, of course, there was the big question—would she still have the ability to think and to remember her family, her friends, and her former life?

Naturally, I wanted to be there when she woke up; but I was exhausted and my two youngest girls needed their mother to be home with them. So Terry was the one who went to Salt Lake. When he arrived, she was beginning to wake up. A few days later, I was able to join Terry to assess how Julene was doing.

At first it was difficult to appraise Julene's mental state. Julene was not able to speak aloud since no air passed by her vocal chords because of the trach. Reading lips was difficult, especially for me. (I never got good at reading lips—unless I already knew what she was going to say!) Writing was incredibly difficult since her muscles had atrophied. But SHE KNEW US! We could talk to her again; we could tell her how much we loved her.

A few days after she was awake, we gave her the cute teddy bear that the Ricks College Personnel Office had sent to her. Her vision was very cloudy, so it was difficult for her to distinguish much of anything. She felt this slender teddy bear, with its long funny legs, and motioned for pencil and paper. With difficulty, she named him "PADDINGTON!" When her nurse returned to the room, she expressed joy and relief: "Oh, she can still think and remember things!"

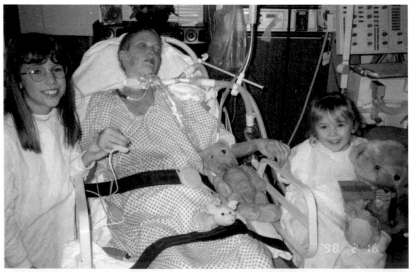

Anneli, Julene, Paddington, Audra, and Honeybear - 2/16/1998

How grateful we were for Julene to be awakened from this coma, to be with us, and to know her mind was still alert. Gratefully, she said she had no memory of anything that had happened while in the induced coma. It was certainly a reminder of the resurrection—except at that time, we will be "re-awakened" in a perfect form.

"Therefore, all things shall be restored to their proper order, every thing to its natural frame" (Alma 41: 4).

MIRACLE #8
THE MIRACLE OF MUSIC

Knowing that music helps the brains of children, we felt that having beautiful classical music playing in the background would be good for Julene, even though she was in an induced coma. But even more impressive was the fact that a kind young musician named Glenn came to the University of Utah Hospital, and visited the rooms of patients, playing guitar and singing for them.

The first time Glenn came to Julene's room, we informed him that there was a good chance that she could not hear him, because of the medication. He chose to play and sing for her anyway. He performed an American folk song, "Oh Susannah," something we had done Bluegrass style for the Folk Dancers.

Glenn came back periodically, and when he realized we would be comfortable with LDS music, he began to play and sing songs from the LDS Children's Song Book. After Julene was conscious, Glenn came on a Sunday when Julene was particularly low, truly feeling hopeless. Glenn chose to sing the Primary song that starts: "Heavenly Father, are you really there? And do you hear and answer every child's prayer . . ." She began to cry—real tears, which was quite unusual for her. She was so grateful for that song, on that day, at that particular moment. She had to wonder day after day if Heaven Father had heard her prayers! Glenn stayed and played two or three other songs for her. It really helped her get through a very difficult day.

Here are the complete lyrics to "A Child's Prayer" by Janice Kapp Perry:

1. Heavenly Father, are you really there?
And do you hear and answer ev'ry child's prayer?
Some say that heaven is far away,
But I feel it close around me as I pray.
Heavenly Father, I remember now
Something that Jesus told disciples long ago:
"Suffer the children to come to me."
Father, in prayer I'm coming now to thee.

2. Pray, he is there; Speak, he is list'ning.
You are his child;
His love now surrounds you.
He hears your prayer;
 He loves the children.
Of such is the kingdom, the kingdom of heav'n.

("A Child's Prayer," *Children's Songbook,* 12–13)
A Child's Prayer © 1984 Janice Kapp Perry. Used by Permission.

Glenn helped Julene again, a year after she left the burn center. In April of 1999, he sent her a CD of songs he had written, with him singing and playing guitar. He wrote a beautiful letter, explaining how touched he had been by her and her beautiful spirit:

Julene, Whenever I think of you, I think of the words courage and long-suffering. Courage is not the absence of fear, but the doing of what we must in spite of fear or intense pain. I recall the Savior's prayer: "Father if it be Thy will, remove this cup from me, nevertheless, thy will be done." That was courage. That was and is power and love. So when I remember you, Julene, I think of the Savior and the Atonement. It has been said that all things bear record of the Savior. You do. And from this I have found courage of my own when faced with fear. Thank you.

40

I wrote the following to Glenn:

When we got home (from Salt Lake), we read your beautiful letter and listened to your CD. It made me cry—to think that we had even affected one person in such a way. I know many people know of her, many pray for her. I do hope her beautiful way with people will help others see the gospel of Jesus Christ in her life. . . Thanks again for your service to so many, and the spirit you share with others."

"For my soul delighteth in the song of the heart; yea, the song of the righteous is a prayer unto me, and it shall be answered with a blessing upon their heads" (D&C 25: 12).

THE TRAUMA (AND DRAMA) CONTINUED

Although we saw significant improvement, January and the following few months were filled with trauma and fear, all in the name of progress. Another surgery took place on January 6. A skin graft was taken from her right leg to close the abdominal wound opened so she could breathe better. After the skin graft healed, she was taken to a huge bath tub called a Hubbard tank. Here she experienced her first bath since the reaction. This was both wonderful and extremely scary, as it required a transfer to a gurney which lowered her partially into the water.

The real trauma came when it was time to start learning to breathe on her own. This was done in several steps. At first, they changed the setting on her ventilator to CPAP (Continuous Positive Airway Pressure) for 10 minutes, then 15 minutes twice a day. She had to learn to use her breathing muscles again because they were so atrophied. It progressed to having her oxygen delivered by a cannula (or tube) that was under her nose. But each of these steps brought incredible fear and fatigue.

Physical therapy was necessary since her muscles had not been used for more than two months. It is an important part of the recovery process for a burn patient. Although Julene wasn't burned by fire, her body was damaged in many of the same ways. Physical therapists helped her relearn the use of her muscles. It was so tiring that seemingly insignificant activities overwhelmed her. Just sitting up in a chair was hard. When they had her dangle her feet off the side of the bed, they started with only five minutes. When they increased it to seven minutes later in the day, it was so difficult that she broke down and cried.

On January 31, they had her stand for the first time, right next to her bed. It was a particularly traumatic situation because the young resident doctor thought they should leave her oxygen at the lower resting level rather than increasing it. I argued that Dr. Saffle, the head doctor at the burn center, said her oxygen could be turned up when she asked for more; but the resident doctor would not bend. It was so incredibly difficult; her knees buckled, and her heart rate soared. Julene was terrified and crying. Dr. Saffle came later and apologized, indicating that the oxygen should have been turned up for the increased activity. Being pushed so hard had a measurable negative physical effect, particularly a very fast heartbeat. But the emotional effect was devastating. I recorded: "Her heart was actually hurting, and she was a basket case inside." She continued to experience emotions that made her feel like she was going crazy.

Another disappointment came when her fiancé, Scott, who had come almost daily while Julene was unconscious, came less often—perhaps twice a week. Then, on Valentine's Day he came with a roommate; he did not have a valentine. Julene then recognized things were different between them. This undoubtedly added to her emotional distress, but she kept her thoughts private. Scott did visit occasionally, but, upon his father's suggestion, moved on with his life.

MIRACLE #9
THE MIRACLE OF HABIT

Although the main emphasis for physical therapy was to have Julene do activities to strengthen her lungs and prepare her to walk again, they needed her to do other things as well. Although her arms had been in a stretched position at night, her arms were still inflexible, unable to open wide.

To give Julene an activity that would help her use her arms and fingers again, we bought her a guitar with a short neck. She started playing guitar in eighth grade, so she had played for eight years and was very good. We wondered if she would still be able to regain her skills. Even with this smaller guitar, it was difficult because at first the left arm could not reach back far enough for the left-hand fingers to form the patterns to play chords or even melodies. Because she loved music and loved the guitar, she was determined to win this battle. This was "physical therapy" she really wanted to do! The staff was thrilled to see the progress she made. `

After a few weeks, we brought her full-sized guitar for her to try. Again, she could not reach back far enough at first, but she gained flexibility. Before long, she tried playing her banjo—and the neck on it is even longer. She had to play it off to the right side in order to reach all the way back on the left side. But because of muscle memory, she was soon able to play difficult guitar passages and complicated banjo breaks even after months of not using her arms and hands.

Before she left the burn center, she played her banjo for some of the nurses and staff. This was truly a miracle. They could see how their dedication in caring for Julene had made an important difference in her life. Being able to make music again made Julene so happy. Months later, after going home, she actually performed at Ricks College on two different occasions. The first was to play banjo with her sister Carla, at the graduation dinner for the Division of Agricultural and Biological Science. They played three songs, including "Dueling Banjos," which is quite a difficult banjo piece. The second occasion was playing with our family Bluegrass Band for a 20-minute show the summer of 1999. It was certainly a sign of improvement that Julene had the physical strength and ability to breathe off the ventilator for this outing which, including transport, took over an hour.

We often think about "habit" as a negative trait, such as our bad habits. But one of our habits is truly miraculous—the habit of muscle memory. This was a beautiful miracle as Julene began to play her string instruments again.

"It is by the exercise of our mental faculties that we improve upon them; it is by the exercise of our physical powers that we strengthen them" (Heber J. Grant, *Conference Report*, April 1945, 5).

MORE IMPROVEMENT IN THE BURN CENTER

On February 17, Julene "graduated!" She was moved from an open room next to the nursing station in the burn center, to a corner room which was bigger and had a door that could be closed. This was an indication that she was more stable and didn't need to be watched so carefully. It also allowed us to have a little more activity without disturbing other patients. She was able to "watch" movies (perhaps listen would be more appropriate, as she could not really see), and she was allowed more than two visitors at the same time since it didn't disrupt the staff or their duties.

Walking and breathing continued to be primary goals. To actually walk somewhere, Julene had to be on a cannula—with the oxygen being delivered through her nose and with her breathing on her own. Julene walked for the first time on February 26; she walked 12-15 feet. Margo was there, but I missed her first walk because I had gone home for President David A. Bednar's Inaugural Celebration at Ricks College. My college bluegrass class was invited to perform and both our daughter, Carla, and Terry's niece, Angela, were playing and singing. It was a success and the audience loved our part of the show.

I wrote in my journal entry of March 5: "Julene had enough strength that she walked to the physical therapy room. There she briefly rode a stationary bike. Later in the day, she also played her banjo."

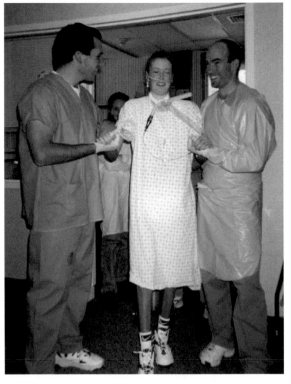

By late February and early March, Julene was on a cannula for several hours each day. On March 10, she stayed off the ventilator all night long, with blow-by oxygen, rather than a cannula. But with these signs of progress came set-backs. She was plagued with low levels of oxygen saturation. By March 16, she was back on the ventilator part of the day and at night.

As Julene continued to make progress, it was necessary for her to be transferred to a rehabilitation center. This was difficult as most rehab centers were not able to take care of a ventilated patient who needed high amounts of oxygen. There was also an issue of funding. At some point, Julene's medical bills maxed out her million-dollar insurance policy, and other arrangements had to be made before a hospital would accept Julene as a patient.

CHAPTER SEVEN
SALT LAKE REGIONAL MEDICAL CENTER AND
MIRACLES TEN THROUGH FIFTEEN

It was decided to move Julene to Salt Lake Regional's Rehabilitation Center because the doctor there was willing to take a ventilated patient. The transfer was made on April 9, 1998. Julene was able to be off the ventilator for part of the day, which meant that the oxygen was just blowing into a cuff over the trachea opening. At night and at times when she was either sick or particularly tired, she was put back on the ventilator. She still needed to have secretions suctioned from her bronchial tubes often. The change to a different hospital was very difficult. With less staff available to help Julene, we were given the responsibility for suctioning her and monitoring her oxygen levels. We helped her with eating, drinking, and personal care procedures. One nurse told me that they would not have been able to keep her if one of us hadn't stayed with her all the time. We were given the hospital bed next to her so we could spend the night there.

Although we were thrilled with Julene's improvement and even her appearance, those who saw her for the first time were shocked. I remember one worker being appalled at how "bad" she looked, saying: "This was the result of penicillin?" I assured her she was looking very good, compared to what she looked like at first.

When Terry's father died in May, we had to make arrangements for others to come be with Julene while we were in Rexburg for the funeral. Scott's grandmother, still supporting us, volunteered to sit with Julene, and arranged for a couple of her friends to also take a turn. Although this wonderful grandmother had heard many details about Julene from the very beginning, she was still shocked to actually see how incredibly difficult life was for Julene.

MIRACLE # 10
THE MIRACLE OF KINDNESS

The nurses at the Rehab Center were especially considerate and caring. Even though there was not enough staff to attend to Julene as constantly as the nurses in the burn center had, many of the nurses here soon loved Julene and did special things for her. One nurse was a beautician and offered to trim Julene's hair. It had finally grown out a couple of inches, but the ends were kinky—and almost black rather than blonde. The nurse brought her shears and stayed after her shift to give Julene a very becoming haircut.

Although I don't remember all the little daily acts of kindness, I do remember the effect their sweet way had on Julene. Her wariness at changing hospitals soon turned to a new confidence. She reflected their love and concern.

Later, at Julene's passing, the staff sent us a lovely card. One of the nurses, with whom she was especially close, sent a beautiful and delicate porcelain rose to express her sympathy. It has reminded us of how their kindness helped Julene.

"Put on therefore, as the elect of God, holy and beloved, bowels of mercies, kindness, humbleness of mind, meekness, longsuffering"
(Colossians 3:12).

MIRACLE #11
THE MIRACLE OF NATURE

At the burn center, almost nothing could be used for Julene unless it came from the pharmacy. The only exception was permission to use oils and lotions externally. Before there was a diagnosis of a penicillin reaction, we had tried to find something to heal the rash and blisters. At a health food store, we were introduced to Christopher's, "Complete Bone & Tissue Massage Oil", which was a combination of herbs incorporated into olive oil. [We now refer to this as our "magic oil," because it has such wonderful healing powers for skin.]

After just a few days in the burn center, we began using this oil on Julene's feet. This was the only part of her body that still had skin that was intact, and the only part of her body that we were able to apply oil to. We used the oil liberally, several times a day. Gradually, the skin around her ankles and lower legs began to heal, and we could put oil there. We were soon able to put the oil on the fingers of one of her hands. As more skin healed, we rubbed the oil on more places on her body. The nursing staff was impressed that the healing was taking place from her extremities rather than from the center of her body, which was more typical.

The one place that was not bandaged and still not healing well was her scalp. Her head had been shaved, and there was dried blood and pus all over her head—a horrible sight! One night, a nurse gave me permission to put the oil on her head. I applied the oil twice and left it on. It turned out to be difficult to clean off, but the skin underneath began to heal.

Months later, we used this same oil on the site where a patch of skin was harvested for a skin graft. The site healed so well she did not need the compression bandages usually prescribed to prevent scarring.

One of the benefits of moving to Salt Lake Regional Medical Center was the relaxed rules about using natural products. The physician over the Rehab Center was familiar with herbs and alternative healing methods. We continued to use oils, but we were also allowed to give her a few approved herbs internally. We started giving her slippery elm each morning. It is known to soothe inflamed mucous membranes and build strong tissue. We were also able to give her herbal drops for relaxation and sleep. We found several homeopathic remedies that contributed to her improvement. We felt these all helped in her recovery.

We continued to study the use of natural remedies and used them in the many months that followed. At Julene's last visit to Salt Lake, her pulmonologist said with a bit of surprise: "Her lungs are actually better—and lungs don't heal. But unfortunately, her bronchials are worse." We felt there had been improvement because of the use of the products of nature—carrot juice being one food given to her almost every day.

What a miracle that the gifts of nature, including vegetables and herbs, were given for man's use. We were grateful to the inspired men and women who studied and combined these natural medicines and made them available for use in Julene's healing!

"And again, verily I say unto you, all wholesome herbs God hath ordained for the constitution, nature, and use of man. Every herb in the season thereof, and every fruit in the season thereof; all these to be used with prudence and thanksgiving"
(D&C 89:10-11).

MIRACLE 12
THE MIRACLE OF OPTIMISM

Since the Rehab Center at SLRMC typically did not have patients who were heavily dependent on both a ventilator and such a high amount of oxygen, the Respiratory Department's services were particularly important. Because Julene was off the ventilator during most of the day, she was able to talk by covering the hole in her throat, therefore allowing the air to pass by her vocal cords. This made it easier to communicate with her instead of trying to read her lips.

Three of the respiratory therapists were young—fairly close to Julene's age. All three of them went the "extra mile" for Julene. They all assured her she was getting better and soon would be back to living a normal life.

One was Rob, a tall young man with dark hair. He brought his guitar and came to her room to sing and play for her. He kept in touch by email when Julene was transferred home.

The second was Jon, a young man with Cystic Fibrosis. He was about 25 years old. He could relate to Julene in a very personal way because he had physical limitations that would undoubtedly get worse as years went by. He, too, would come sit by Julene, offering encouragement. Sometimes he held her hands. Once he brought her a flower—probably from the hospital's rose garden. Another time, he danced with her. One special day, he brought her a little brown teddy bear from the gift shop that she named "Brownie."

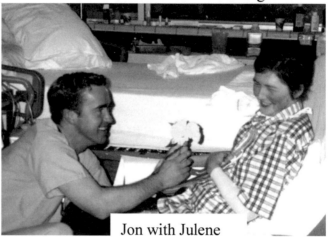
Jon with Julene

The third respiratory therapist was Teresa, a darling single girl who had so much energy that her enthusiasm for life was contagious. She

Teresa - Rob - Jon with Julene

50

had a great sense of humor and was quite a tease. Sometimes when she was between assignments or in the late evening, she would sit by Julene's bedside and they would talk. They soon became as close as sisters.

One afternoon, both Jon and Teresa were with Julene. They had a little contest. Teresa fanned Julene and her oxygen saturation (SATs) went up. Then Jon fanned her and her SATSs went down—and that was on 100% oxygen. Julene really laughed heartily for the first time that I could remember since the reaction.

Julene kept in touch with these three special individuals. She emailed them letters. At first, she would dictate the letter, and I would type it. But as she got more strength and mobility, she wrote a few of the letters herself. Here is one of the best, just as she typed it:

The Top Ten Reasons to Notice that I'm Getting Well

10 ~ I am typing this list myself (at a font size of 46 points).
9 ~ I can eat solid foods such as macaroni and cheese, bread, and cold cereal!
8 ~ I can put my hair in a ponytail.
7 ~ I can count six eyelashes instead of four.
6 ~ I take a bath in the bathtub once a week, whether I need it or not. :)
5 ~ My Optometrist suggested that I shave my legs!!
4 ~ Only half my doctors make house calls (instead of all).
3 ~ I make telephone calls and actually do some talking instead of just clicking!
2 ~ I made my first non-medical field trip to accompany Carla as she played and sang for her Division Banquet. I played the guitar or banjo on 3 numbers.
And the **Number One** Reason to Notice that I'm getting better . . .
I can tell that I am a girl!

JULENE -- April 10, 1999

These three individuals gave Julene the encouragement she needed to start healing, but I think she was a miracle in their lives as much as they were in hers.

"We need those who bring gladness into our lives. We need those who give encouragement and reflect optimism" (Marvin J. Ashton, "A Voice of Gladness" *Ensign,* May 1991).

MIRACLE #13
THE MIRACLE OF CHARITY AND VISITING TEACHERS

At the Rehab Center, visiting teachers were assigned to come on a weekly basis. The first time a visiting teacher came, she only stood in the doorway of the room and said: "We are your visiting teachers. Is there anything we can do for you today?" I thanked her for coming but did not know what she could do. She answered: "Okay, we'll see you next month." Then she left.

The next week a sister came, apparently from a different ward. She came into the room, visited, and learned a little about the situation. She came back another time and assisted with the wheelchair, so Julene could go down to the rose gardens. She invited me to stay at her home if I needed a place to stay.

Another week a sister from yet a different ward came. She spent 30 minutes getting to know Julene and learning about her reaction to penicillin. She was appalled at the terrible consequences, and she was extremely concerned for Julene's present situation. It is remarkable how many good things happened as a result of her one visit.

This sister went back to her Relief Society and reported the heart-breaking situation of a twenty-one-year old girl. The Relief Society president came to visit, and then others. The ward held a special fast for

Julene. At that fast and testimony meeting, Sister Olivia King, a member of the Relief Society general board, was a visitor. Sister King felt impressed to visit Julene. She and her husband brought the beautiful red tulips from the podium and headed for the hospital. She became a special friend to Julene, visiting often when Julene was in Salt Lake. She sent cards, letters, and emails when we were home in Rexburg.

At the next Relief Society general board meeting, Sister King told Julene's story. President Mary Ellen Smoot took time out of her busy schedule to visit Julene. On her second visit, she brought a beautiful, peach-colored quilt with lace to comfort Julene. On this occasion, she told Julene: "You will probably use your experiences to help others someday. You might have a position like I have." (Although Julene never had the privilege of speaking of her experiences during her earthly sojourn, many were inspired by her faith, bravery, and perseverance.)

Another person who participated in this special fast for Julene was Dr. N. Branson Call, the doctor who later performed a surgery on Julene's eyelids. When he met Julene, he realized that she was the same girl for whom their ward had fasted some weeks earlier.

This miracle of charity began with one caring visit by a Relief Society sister who inspired others. It was like the pebble thrown into a pond—the ripples continue all the way to the shore. It had a profound effect on Julene and our entire family.

"And above all things, clothe yourselves with the bond of charity, as with a mantle, which is the bond of perfectness and peace."
(D&C 88:125).

MIRACLE #14
THE MIRACLE OF EMPATHY

Although there were many good things about Julene's move to the Rehab Center, there was a downside. Some of the physical therapists did not understand how severely Julene's body had been damaged and that she really could not do all they were requiring. This was especially true when she was off the ventilator. There were several times they did not listen when she complained she wasn't getting any oxygen. They would answer by saying, "You are fine." Once when Terry was with her, he said: "But her oxygen tank shows it is on empty!" Another time, when she protested, she was hooked to a wall fixture—however, there was no oxygen in that dispenser.

Perhaps the most disturbing situation was that two young female physical therapists talked to each other as if she were not even present, sometimes even talking about her. Margo spent the afternoon with Julene on April 22, 1998, while I was home giving finals. Margo objected to the physical therapists' treatment of Julene and reported that one lady in particular was rude, insistent, and impatient. Physical therapy became emotionally difficult, as well as physically exhausting, day after day.

After the next care-conference, Julene was reassigned to an energetic physical therapist named Tim Semadeni. As he worked with Julene, he tried to understand her capability and her limitations when breathing, especially while participating in physical activities. He cared enough to exercise at home for 30 minutes while breathing through a straw—which would be similar to Julene breathing through her constricted and damaged tracheal tubes.

Tim was able to talk to Julene, encourage her, tease her, and entertain her while she was doing physical activities that were so difficult for her. One day he told this funny story: "I was in the elevator with several others when two nurses got on the elevator. I greeted them and said: 'It's nice to see you in your clothes!' (Of course, meaning not in scrubs.) I got some very strange looks from the visitors in the elevator!" Tim made her laugh in the midst of physical therapy when before she so often cried.

Because Tim truly understood her limitations, he listened to her needs. She gained strength by walking further, riding a bicycle longer, walking up an incline, and increasing the time she could do other physical activities. Their last goal, and requirement for her to go home, was for her to be able to climb five stairs. We all celebrated when this was accomplished.

It was because of the miracle of empathy that Julene made such wonderful progress with Tim.

"And whether one member suffer, all the members suffer with it; or one member be honoured, all the members rejoice with it"
(1 Corinthians 12:26).

MIRACLE #15
BLESSING OF SUFFERING ENDURED

The primary goal at the Rehab Center was to help Julene breathe well enough to go home. It became apparent that she would need to be ventilated at night time. They experimented with different portable ventilators. Of course, this turned out to be difficult. Apparently, all ventilators do not deliver air in exactly the same manner. With one vent, Julene complained that her neck hurt. When I checked her oxygen saturation, it had dropped to 68 percent. (Below 88 was unacceptable, and below 70 was dangerous.) As a result, her anxiety was so great she was given the drug, Ativan. At least two more ventilators were tried, but neither met her needs. The focus was changed to building up her strength, hoping she would not need a ventilator.

At the burn center, there was a schedule of spending more time each day using the cannula. At Salt Lake Regional, however, the pulmonologist decided she should just be put on a cannula for a few days, without gradually working up to it. While I was home on Saturday, May 16, they took out her trach tube, (which meant they couldn't put her back on the ventilator), and left her on a cannula, breathing on her own. Both of her primary doctors were gone over the weekend, so it was just the respiratory staff who were left to care for her breathing needs. She became exhausted, but no one was able to change the orders. Terry said it was terrible to watch, and he was glad I wasn't there. By Sunday, her oxygen had dropped dangerously low, and her CO2 had risen to 112—with the normal being 30 to 40. Terry had dozed off and woke suddenly when alarms were going off. There were four staff members attending her. He didn't tell me this at the time, but he was sure she had quit breathing. To put her back on a ventilator, she had to be intubated—

which means the tube is put into the mouth and into the trachea. At first, it was not placed correctly and the air from the vent was going out through her mouth rather than going to her lungs properly. That 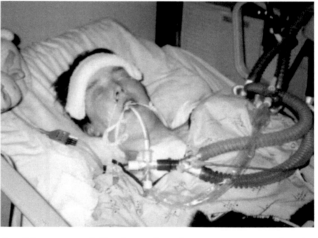 was corrected, but she had become dehydrated and was, once again, in critical condition. She was taken to ICU. It was five days before she was stable enough to be taken to surgery and have a new trach tube inserted.

By the time I came back on May 19th, she had a <u>resting</u> heart rate of 150 beats per minute, which was double the normal rate. Her clothing and bedding were soaking wet. The next day, the pulmonologist on call said that, according to the X-rays, she had pneumonia. They discussed antibiotics, and I reminded them: "NO PENICILLIN!" Julene, still intubated and unable to talk, pointed to her ears, meaning: "No antibiotics that harm the ears." The doctor later thanked me for being there, because of the two drugs he first considered, one was a relative of penicillin and the other was potentially damaging to the ears. The antibiotic, Ciprofloxacin was administered and after 2-3 hours, Julene finally smiled—but only one time.

The tracheostomy was done on May 22nd and was painful. It required a lot of pain medication as well as sedation. After lots of coughing and feeling very stressed, Julene said: "I can use my mouth." (Because she had been in the induced coma when she was intubated originally, she had not experienced being "gag-tied," and it was a horrific experience for her.)

In my journal entry for Saturday, May 23rd, I wrote: "Julene has adjusted some to the new trach. She asked me, 'What if I'm not pretty again?' I tried to reassure her. Just then Dr. Parkinson walked in and said: 'Julene—you look so beautiful!' He introduced Julene to his wife, and then his son played the flute for us. He left a prescription to help her skin heal more. Julene seemed much more like herself after the Parkinsons' visit." I also wrote that a friend came with a ham dinner, which was quite an unexpected treat. In my journal I said, "Julene ate a little bread and ham. She seemed to swallow more easily."

Julene's blood gas test, (which measures both oxygen and CO2 content), was done later that Saturday night. The results were really quite encouraging. However, by Sunday morning, Julene was having a very difficult time again. She just cried and cried. I went down to her room in Rehab to get something, and on the way back I was trying to figure out why Julene couldn't quit crying. A very distinct thought came into my mind: "She's having morphine withdrawal." When I got back to the ICU, Julene said: "Why am I so cold? And yet I am sweating!" I thought that might be part of the morphine withdrawal as well.

We watched the BYU broadcast of a Church service, and we were both crying when the pulmonologist came into the room. He worked with the ventilator settings and that seemed to make her more comfortable.

After such a catastrophic week, Julene was definitely in need of some cheer! It came in the form of visitors. Ron Andrus, her friend from bluegrass band, called from Brigham City to see if he could visit. So, Julene fixed up a little—and that's hard to do in an ICU gown!

During the hour it took Ron to drive from Brigham City, our neighbors, Sander and Merlyn Larson arrived. Sander was the Ricks College administrator who helped bluegrass band become a class, and he had watched over Julene for almost four years! Still another visitor came—one of her favorite physical therapists from the burn center came with his wife. Then our oldest daughter SaraLyn came unexpectedly. With so many friends to cheer her, some of the horrible depression lessened.

When Ron arrived, he stayed quite a long time. Ron was a really good friend—like the brother our girls never had. He was often in our home for rehearsals, for meals, and just to be there. A favorite story will illustrate how close he was to our family, and why this visit was so meaningful.

At the beginning of Julene's sophomore year, Ron asked her to go to a movie. She said she couldn't because she was taking care of her baby sister. He said, "Let's just take her with us." One of Julene's friends who had moved away was back in Rexburg and saw the three of them. She said: "Julene, I didn't know you had a baby!" Julene, still only 18 years old, answered: "I do—I have a baby sister." Ron loved playing the part of being there with a baby!

On this visit, Ron had brought his guitar and he played and sang a couple of numbers. I brought Julene her banjo, and together they played and Ron sang "Callin' Baton Rouge." He gave her a blessing before he left.

The next day was Memorial Day, and that meant not having such a rigid schedule. They let us sleep until 9:00!! Unfortunately, Julene still cried and cried, and nothing cheered her. Jon, her new friend from Respiratory, tried to chase her gloom away. She was so despondent she asked him: "Am I going to live?" Seeing Julene so disheartened again, I finally asked a nurse to get her Ativan, a sedative to relieve anxiety.

Amazingly, when she needed friends so much, they again came unannounced on this holiday. Two of the physical therapists from the burn center came with their wives. It was so fun to have them back teasing Julene again. While they talked about old times, they stretched her ham strings and her elbow extensions. They even checked to see if the scars on her arms had healed. They stayed almost an hour.

After the Memorial Day weekend, there were talks with the two regular doctors. It was hard to appreciate the doctor who put her on a cannula and then left town. It felt like he had left her to die. Oddly, I don't remember the conference I had with him, but I did record it in a fair amount of detail in my journal:

> The doctor admitted: 'I take full responsibility for that weekend. I really thought she could do it and she couldn't.' I told him about her emotional low, the morphine withdrawal, and her depression. I asked why he didn't do breathing trials with Julene like they had done at the burn center. He said: 'It's not my style.' He then said: 'I gather that you haven't been pleased with my service.' I compared our experience to the burn center with ever present doctors. Maybe we expected too much and that maybe we were just lucky that he would treat Julene. He answered: 'I think so. And I haven't charged a penny for it, because it was such a sad case.' Earlier he said, her sad condition has touched everyone in this hospital who has seen her. I told him I was sorry if I was too critical and he said: 'It is okay—you are a mother.'

Julene suffered so much during the last two weeks of May of 1998, it was truly hard to understand. Almost miraculously, she survived! Gratefully we recognized the tender mercies of her friends who chose to come at this low point in her life. But we have also come to understand that one gains a fellowship with our Savior, Jesus Christ, through suffering. We knew she had a personal testimony of the divinity of our Elder Brother, Jesus Christ, and she understood more than most, how He suffered in our behalf.

"My son, peace be unto thy soul; thine adversity and thine afflictions shall be but a small moment; And then, if thou endure it well, God shall exalt thee on high; thou shalt triumph over all thy foes."
(D&C: 121:7-8)

SAYING GOOD-BYE TO THE REHAB CENTER

In early June, a brand-new ventilator became available. It was ordered, delivered, and tested. We had just experienced another miracle! This vent did all we needed it to do! It was portable, it ran on a battery, and it could be plugged into a 12-volt system when used in the car.

Julene's release date was scheduled for Friday, June 12, 1998. It was exactly one year—to the day, that we had performed our concert for the Ricks College Summer Entertainment Series. So much had changed in one year.

Friday was the day all the physical therapy patients met together in a large room. Julene was the only young person with a group of senior citizens who were in the Rehab Center. Usually, Julene was taken to this activity in her wheelchair. But on this, her last day, Tim, her physical therapist, decided she should do something fun. She put her giant teddy bear, Bubba, in the wheelchair, and she pushed him into the room. The patients waiting there were so amused and happy to see Julene doing something so clever. They were thrilled to know she was well enough to go home.

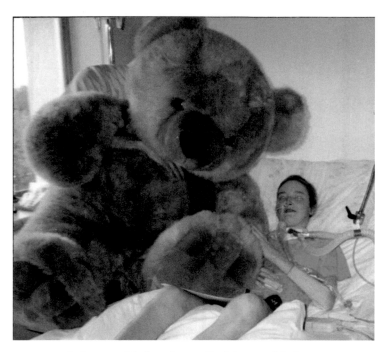

Julene with her bear, Bubba, a gift from
her Uncle Keith and Aunt Sandy

On June 12, 1998, we packed her belongings, her new ventilator, and tanks of oxygen into our van. When Julene finished physical therapy, she said good-bye to all her new friends, and we took her down to our van. Sister Olivia King was there to tell her farewell and to send a few snacks for the ride home. She took a picture so we could remember this long-awaited day. We left Salt Lake about 3 p.m. and arrived home at 8:45. We were so thankful to have Julene well enough to leave the hospital and to be back in our home!

CHAPTER EIGHT
HOME TO REXBURG AND
MIRACLES SIXTEEN AND SEVENTEEN

Being home was not as easy as we had imagined. Yes, we had oxygen tanks and a hospital bed, but we were now her sole caretakers! Julene was scared being home. Although we thought she would sleep better in a quiet home, she still struggled to go to sleep. We assumed she would want to come to the table for meals, but that overwhelmed her. She needed help to get out of bed both because she was weak and because she needed help to manage her feeding and oxygen tubes.

There was so much to do all the time. It took a few days before we had a home-health nurse, who came two or three days a week, and an aide who came on the other days. While Julene gained strength in one area, she experienced adverse reactions in other ways.

Julene had been throwing up every morning for a long time. She had been given the antidepressant Zoloft while at SLRMC. I forgot to give it to her on July 5, and she didn't throw up. After identifying the connection, her doctor said to stop the Zoloft. Although this stopped her throwing up, extreme depression set in and was very difficult to counteract. There were several days that Julene did not want to do anything, did not care about anything, did not want to even live.

Each day was a series of suctioning her secretions, which meant a tube was inserted into the tracheotomy and the build-up of mucus was pulled out with a suctioning machine. She was still on the ventilator at night; but in the morning, we changed her over to a cannula. It was necessary to turn up the oxygen level when she got up to walk, to change rooms, or to use the commode.

We had to manage the food pump and her feeding tube, which delivered a liquid diet as well as medicine and supplements. When infection set in, she was given antibiotics—some of which she had allergic reactions to. The effect of any antibiotic was a build-up of yeast and digestive tract discomfort. By July 20, she was so sick we talked seriously about taking her to the Idaho Falls Hospital. However, the next day she turned a corner and things were better.

To complicate matters, it turned hot, and Julene was suffering from the increased heat. We tried taking her downstairs where it was cool, but the trip up and down the stairs was grueling for her. Terry contacted an air conditioning company and explained our needs. The company came the next day. Thankfully, Julene was able to be more comfortable in about two days' time.

MIRACLE #16
THE MIRACLE OF SERVICE

Julene, writing her own story, penned: *"In the days of modern transportation, the doctor that would make a house call has almost become a legend—except at my house! My medical condition, my physical condition—to be more specific, kept me homebound, even bedridden at times. So, if I needed medical attention, the doctor had to come to us."*

Hans Redd, M. D., agreed to be Julene's physician in Rexburg. When we were making arrangements to bring Julene home, he said: "Your house is halfway between my house and my office. I can stop and see her there." He was amazing and the perfect doctor for Julene. He understood her needs, he was kind, he made good decisions for her care, and he always came when Julene needed him. We will always be thankful for his great gift of service.

Another great act of service was performed by a physical therapist from Idaho Falls. Todd Storms, P.T., came four times a week for several months. Although Julene was on a Medicare program which allowed payment for physical therapy, he never charged for his time. He said: "I have gained so much from being with Julene that I do not want to be paid for coming here." He had a beautiful gold necklace made that had a holograph of her picture etched into it. He gave it to me the day we did Julene's temple ordinances one year after she died. It is one of my most precious keepsakes.

63

Because of the cloudiness of her cornea, Julene was not able to see more than just shapes. She could not talk very well because of the tracheostomy and the ventilator. But when the day came when she could hardly hear, she thought she would go crazy—literally. She was so depressed and so anxious that we found Dr. Grant Davis, an Ears, Nose, and Throat Specialist in Rexburg, who agreed to see her almost immediately. He found that her ears had filled with tissue and wax that was so thick it had impaired her hearing. He cleaned her ears and her hearing was restored. But as we talked about a future appointment, he said: "I'll come to your house—it is too difficult to bring her here!"

Our optometrist, Dr. Scott Mortensen, had worked with our entire family—since I am terribly near-sighted and passed those genes on to all six of our daughters. So it was not surprising that he was willing to come to our house, except when he needed to use the equipment in his office. About every two weeks, he came to remove the wild eyelashes that kept growing right into Julene's eye. But it was his willingness to come one day at 7 a.m. that proved to be most crucial. She was in excruciating pain, and upon examination, he could see that her cornea was failing. His timeliness undoubtedly helped save her eye.

Doctors from Salt Lake even came to our house. Dr. N. Branson Call was coming to a clinic in Idaho Falls and then continued up to Rexburg with his wife. We all had dinner together at our house. Afterward, we played "Balderdash." This game could be done without her having to see very much, and Julene thought of very clever responses. While there, he removed stitches that were placed in the eyelid surgery he performed two weeks earlier. Both her eye and eyelid looked good.

Surprisingly, Dr. Nathan Dean, her very busy pulmonologist from LDS Hospital, visited Julene when he came to Rexburg in the company of his two sons. An anesthesiologist from Salt Lake also stopped to see Julene. But this visit probably doesn't count because he was related by marriage to Julene's oldest sister, SaraLyn. It was mostly a social call, but he cared enough to see how she was doing following the surgery at which he assisted.

There were other Salt Lake doctors who said they would have come to Rexburg, but the opportunity never presented itself. It was heart-warming to know they were willing.

Another volunteer never to be forgotten was Linda Barnes. She was a "Zonologist," which is a person who has been trained in the art of healing by stimulating pressure points in the feet. Linda came for an hour twice a week for several months and never accepted payment. Julene always felt better after Linda worked on her feet. Besides, she was always so positive and happy. When she finished the "zone," she would always say: "There—now you are perfect!" (The added benefit of getting to know Linda was that she arranged a blind date for Margo with her neighbor's son, and now he is my son-in-law!)

These many acts of service helped Julene know that there were professionals who were willing to give of their time to help her heal. We thank them still.

"When ye are in the service of your fellow beings ye are only in the service of your God." (Mosiah 2:17)

IMPORTANT VISITOR

The first part of August continued with a few good days, but most days she had some kind of crisis, usually related to her inability to breathe. She had a few visitors, but most neighbors were uncomfortable coming. Many of her friends had moved on with their lives and were not around to visit.

We heard that Merrill J. Bateman, the President of Brigham Young University, was scheduled to come to Rexburg to speak at the Ricks College Devotional. Because President Bateman had accompanied the BYU Folk Dancer tour, he knew Julene and Margo. Julene asked me to contact President Bateman's office directly. The reply from President Bateman's secretary was that this message had been sent to Ricks

College: "Make whatever changes that are necessary, but I want to visit Julene." On August 19, 1998, President Bateman came to our home and visited with Julene. President Bateman then gave Julene a beautiful blessing.

MIRACLE #17
THE MIRACLE OF A FRIEND

Most of Julene's friends supported her through this lengthy illness, but when a person is hospitalized for a long period of time, is unable to breathe without a machine, is unable to speak aloud, is unable to walk unencumbered, and looks totally different, some friends fall into the shadows. She had one in particular one who was a "fair-weather friend." He had been invited to a party at our house by a mutual friend. They ate snacks and played games around the kitchen table. Afterward, he told his friend that he did not want to come again. His reason was: "I did not like seeing her like that." The young man who planned the party said, "But she is the same on the inside!" Unfortunately, this friend never returned.

Another young man, Jared Benedict, had been friends with Julene in High School. He began visiting her every Sunday evening. He would sit beside her and hold her hand. She would usually be off the ventilator so she could actually talk to him, but he was also good at reading lips. They would laugh and joke. This was one of the highlights of the summer of 1998. It was sad that her vision was so clouded over because he was VERY good looking!

Anneli, Julene, Audra, and Jared

While at home, Julene had been able to eat soft foods, and she could drink—especially juices that were a little thicker. We started juicing carrots, as they were touted as the most healing of the vegetable juices, especially for lung disorders. After several weeks, we noticed bits of orange in the secretions we suctioned from her bronchial tubes. It became more noticeable, with little fibers of carrots showing. It was decided that she had thrown up so much (due to the depression medicine) that the stomach acids had worn a hole in the tissue between the esophagus and the tracheal tubes. However, in late August, something went terribly wrong with her breathing. It appeared that the ventilator was not able to be effective with that break in the tissue. Julene was admitted to Eastern Idaho Regional Medical Center in Idaho Falls on Sunday, August 30.

This was an extremely difficult change—all Julene wanted to do was return home. In addition, it felt like this hospital was not prepared to take care of someone with as many life-threatening problems and sensitivities as she had. Although we explained that Julene was allergic to albuterol, on Wednesday, September 2, they gave her a bronchodilator which was stronger than albuterol. Julene complained about its effects, but they did not believe the symptoms were caused by this medicine. They administered the drug again on Friday, and this time the reaction was severe. Apparently, her bronchial tubes swelled so much, the vent could not work properly. She was left to breathe on her own. This was so incredibly difficult that it was heart-wrenching to watch her struggle for each breath. She was so scared—scared she couldn't keep breathing! And scared she was going to die! She said the only reason she wanted to keep living was because she loved her family. There were several hours where she couldn't decide whether she wanted to make the effort to live through this horrendous night or not. Terry's stake president from his Ricks College stake came, and together they gave her a priesthood blessing.

That same day, Jared found out that Julene was in the Idaho Falls Hospital. He felt inspired to come spend time with her that evening. He sat with her, reassured her that she could keep breathing, and helped her get through one of the most difficult nights of this ordeal. I had been with her all day and was exhausted and hungry. It was late enough that there was no food available at the hospital. Because Jared was there with her, Julene said it would be all right if both Terry and I left the hospital (for the first time in days) to go buy something to eat.

Without the miracle of Jared's friendship and his understanding of who Julene really was on the inside, Julene may not have survived this night.

"A friend loveth at all times, and a brother is born for adversity."
(Proverbs 17:17)

CHAPTER NINE
LDS HOSPITAL, SALT LAKE CITY

Not knowing how to get the right kind of help for Julene, I called Dr. Parkinson, the doctor from Provo who had taken such special interest in Julene. He said he could arrange a physician to physician transfer. He intended to have her flown to Salt Lake that very evening. However, after visiting with the doctors in Idaho Falls, they decided that she was stable; and because of high winds that night, it would be better to wait until Sunday morning. On Sunday, September 6, she was flown by a fixed-wing plane to Salt Lake City airport where she was transferred to LDS Hospital by ambulance.

After such a frightful few days in Idaho Falls, coming to still another hospital was a difficult adjustment. Her stress surfaced as a very high heartrate. She was immediately thrust into breathing trials, physical therapy, occupational therapy and speech therapy. Her new doctors were wonderful, and the staff was experienced with working with patients with similar problems. However, they came in a variety of personalities. Most were kind, some were fun, others were accommodating and generous, but there were a few who were impatient and difficult to work with. Some either wouldn't listen or didn't believe Julene's feedback. Some felt the only way she would ever get better was if they pushed her past her limit. Unfortunately, with this approach, she almost always digressed. The goal was to help her have the strength to breathe on her own as well as being able to eat entirely by mouth and therefore eliminating the feeding tube. They wanted her to be able to dress alone and be able to communicate better. There was progress, but some of these goals were difficult to achieve because of her poor eyesight due to damage to her eyes. It seemed like there were setbacks at every turn.

Shortly after Julene's arrival at LDS Hospital, she had several visitors. Dr. Parkinson came from Provo to visit her. Elder Dellenbach had been in contact with us when we were still in Idaho Falls, and had again put her name on the First Presidency prayer roll. Now that she was in Salt Lake, he came by to visit. And Sister Olivia King was a frequent visitor who always seemed to know what to do to cheer Julene. She said she felt a special bond with Julene—like they were sisters. Additionally, BYU was back in session so some of Julene's friends from the folk-dance team came to visit. One couple stayed with Julene on Sunday nights when we left   for Rexburg. These visits created a climate of encouragement and optimism.

After about five weeks of intense physical therapy and other activities to help her improve, we were told that Julene's lungs were still so damaged that the only way she could recover was if she had a lung transplant. They informed us that it would be extremely expensive, and a patient is put on a waiting list. It is not done by how serious the need is. Terry said he would mortgage the farm to save Julene. At this time, one of Julene's nurses had worked in a lung transplant division of a hospital. She stressed how hard the procedure was, and how hard the patient had to exercise. She talked about the necessity of taking anti-rejection medicine. After listening to this negative picture, Julene said to me: "I never want to have a lung transplant, and besides, I probably couldn't tolerate all the medicine."

By contrast, Julene had one nurse who gave her the extra-mile treatment she needed. Larry seemed a little crazy, but he had so much experience and really understood her needs. He was also a massage therapist, and sometimes, when she had such terrible headaches, he would do a little bit of massage at pressure points to help relieve the pain. He trusted her judgment about how much she could do because he knew she was trying her best. I was impressed that he even listened to "the mother!" On one occasion Julene had walked outside, and after ten minutes she really struggled to breathe. The next day I told Larry that I had this distinct thought come into my mind this morning: "Julene had a harder time breathing when she was walking outside because she was dehydrated." He thought about this and then increased the amount of fluid she was getting. One Sunday Larry said: "For Julene, I'll even go to church," and he took her to the LDS Services held at the hospital.

When Julene was released from the hospital, he donated his recumbent bicycle, hoping it would help her exercise better.

Julene celebrated her 22ⁿᵈ birthday on October 21, 1998, at LDS Hospital. Her party was held in a nice conference room. Some of her friends from other hospitals came as well as family members. Sister Olivia King came as did President Mary Ellen Smoot and her husband.

Julene's 22ⁿᵈ Birthday -Eileen, Julene, President Mary Ellen W. Smoot, and her husband Stanley M. Smoot.

CHAPTER TEN
HOME AGAIN AND MIRACLES
EIGHTEEN THROUGH TWENTY-ONE

Julene was so happy to be home again. Hospitals are always busy and noisy in the early mornings; but at home, we could let Julene sleep longer since her nights were ALWAYS difficult. The biggest disadvantage was that all of Julene's care was again on our shoulders, and she could never be left alone without a highly trained caregiver!

A typical day for Julene started with suctioning—which meant a tube was inserted into the tracheostomy tubing and the build-up of mucus was pulled out with a suctioning machine. She still was on the ventilator at night; however, in the morning we changed her over to a cannula. We completed morning hygiene procedures in her bedroom, including drops and lubrication for her eyes. Then she walked into our family room which was next to the dining room and kitchen area. Her four-year-old sister, Audra, would usually push the portable oxygen tank she used for this walk.

Julene spent most of the day in a recliner in the family room. We bought a treadmill for her, and she walked twice a day. She walked for five minutes, then rested for several minutes before she walked the second five minutes. By then she was very, very tired. In the early afternoon, a physical therapist came and worked with her for about 30-40 minutes, strengthening her arms and upper body. In the early evening, she would walk again, usually for another ten minutes.

Although Julene was able to swallow some real food, it was difficult. She especially found that drinking water or other thin liquids would make her cough and choke, so we bought drinks similar to nectar. Because she still couldn't eat enough to meet her caloric need, she continued to have a feeding tube. When she was in the induced coma and for many months thereafter, she had an NG (nasogastric) tube, which meant a tube was threaded through her nose to her stomach. The tube was stapled to her face next to her nose. Both canned formula and liquid medications were pumped through this tube. When it became obvious she would never be able to eat sufficient quantities by mouth, she had a surgical procedure to insert a tube into her abdomen, called a PEG—percutaneous endoscopic gastrostomy. It was now easier to meet her nutritional needs, and the tube was bigger and didn't clog as easily. Part of our daily responsibilities was to make sure her feeding bag and the pump were properly providing her with nutrients.

Because Julene was so nearly blind, the Idaho Commission for the Blind and Visually Impaired gave her access to their lending program for books on tape. Although I read aloud several books to Julene, this service allowed her to be entertained while she was resting and I was busy. She listened to many Agatha Christie mysteries and was often able to figure out the culprit about two-thirds of the way through the book! Dorothy L. Sayers' mysteries were not so easy to solve, but always full of fascinating details.

To keep Julene's mind sharp, the Commission for the Blind also sent a braille teacher so Julene could learn to read books in braille. This was a great activity, and although she learned the alphabet and could punch out the letters correctly, reading stories was still beyond her skill level.

Julene continued to play both her guitar and banjo. To help me with my college bluegrass band, I brought home a couple of students and Julene taught them the guitar breaks that had never been written out. She also had two or three banjo students—and I was one of them! Music brought Julene a lot of joy and comfort, and so did those who came to play music with her.

Perhaps the highlight of Julene's day would be the arrival of her aide, Heidi. This wonderful lady did so many extra-special things for Julene. She would brush her hair and fix it in different ways—sometimes in a braid, sometimes with ribbons she had bought on her way. One day she surprised Julene with a new shirt. She was always so cheerful and happy that it was hard to be grumpy around her. She learned to do things exactly like Julene needed and wanted them done.

If Julene felt well enough, she would sit at the table with us for a meal. Since there was so little that she could eat, she often did not feel it was worth the effort of moving. She did come to the computer a few times, but that depended on the condition of her eyes. She also walked into the living room and played the piano on several occasions. She could no longer see the printed page, but her fingers still remembered many songs.

One of her delights was having Audra come sit with her in the recliner or next to her on her bed. Audra learned how to help in several ways, and Julene called her "my four-year-old nurse." She also enjoyed the company of the two or three neighbors who visited on a regular basis.

The evening was a reversal of the morning and would usually take more than two hours. It meant walking back to her room with a small tank of oxygen and being suctioned. She changed from her daytime clothes into a gown, received medications either orally or inhaled, and tried to get comfortable when hooked back up to the ventilator. No matter what we did, it was always very difficult for her to go to sleep. She almost always needed to be suctioned between 3 and 4 a.m., so nights were very short.

MIRACLE #18
MIRACLE OF HUMOR

Julene always had a very keen sense of humor. On her good days, she was able to be fairly positive, and she let her sense of humor shine forth. She loved to spend time with her youngest sister, Audra. She

74

taught her the alphabet and several nursery rhymes. She also wrote a very clever poem that described Audra's habits and activities during this time.

BEDTIME

By Julene Wilcox—November 16, 1999

I cannot go to bed tonight
Said little Audra without spite
here's always just too much to do
And I can't rest until YOU do.

There are supplements to pour and bring
And nursery rhymes that I can sing.
There's carrot juice I've got to make
And calcium I've got to take.

I cannot brush my teeth just yet
I'm hungry still, did you forget?
Oh, can I watch a movie PLEASE
But Dad I want some Cottage Cheese

There's no way that you'll see me yawn
I haven't got my jammies on.
I have to feed the dog again.
Please don't say you'll count to ten!

Oh, mommy get that dollie down
I'll go put on my Pooh nightgown.
I cannot go to sleep it's true
'Til one a.m. or maybe two.

Just one more story, then I'll sleep
(But promises aren't meant to keep.)
I'll just sit down here in your lap,
And maybe take a little nap.
"HELLO—it's morning," Audra said—

"How did I get here in my bed?"

She also wrote a poem about herself. It really described many of the difficult, even tragic things that happened, and yet she could write about them in a clever way. This is presented exactly as she typed it, including the same font.

LIMERICK # 99 by Julene Wilcox

There once was a girl named Julene,
 Who surgically lost her spleen (or was it the gall bladder)
  But now she's just swell,
  Though some days are like heck
'Cuz low oxygen turns her face ~~GREEN~~ (no BLUE)

Last month we went to the BIG CITYYYY
To be thrice a cornea transplantee
  And tho' I'm not blind
  I'm starting to find
That now I just can't quite see.

Julene's favorite "docs" make house calls
To check her, or eat, or just stall.
  So which city can boast
  It sends doctors the most
Rexburg—6, Salt Lake-3, and 2 from Idaho Falls.

So what does one do on a vent?
Lots of time breathing, and coughing is spent
  But I knit and crochet
  And write poems all day
Except when I walk on the treadmill, teach banjo lessons, arrange piano quartets, make decorative "Winnie the Pooh" piñatas, learn to read and write Braille, and listen to the Books on Tape that the State Library has lent!

On her last visit to Salt Lake, she said some very funny things that showed her sense of humor. At LDS Hospital, she was transported to the X-ray Department in a wheelchair. Her ventilator was placed on a second wheel chair alongside of her. The young man who was transporting her said: "Everyone just moves to the side and stares at us." Julene responded: "Well then, it is a good thing I'm nearly blind. Otherwise, I might be embarrassed." Terry and I both laughed, but not knowing Julene, the young man couldn't decide if he should laugh or not.

The next day, Julene had an appointment with Dr. Mark Mifflin. This was a follow-up to the surgery performed a few weeks earlier. He cut the stitches that were holding her eye closed, and looked at her eye. He asked her if she could see. She looked at him and said: "This is the first time I've ever <u>seen</u> you" and to me, her mother: "Mom, it's been a long time since I've <u>seen</u> you."

"A merry heart doeth good like a medicine" (Proverbs 17:22).

MIRACLE #19
THE MIRACLE OF SIGHT

It became apparent a few weeks into her hospitalization, that Julene's eyes were damaged. To keep moisture in the eye tissue, her eyelids were sewn shut while she was in the induced coma. When they stopped the medication that had kept her unconscious until December 26, 1997, they opened the eyelids. When she was able to communicate, she said she couldn't see and explained that it was like looking through waxed paper.

The burn center doctors brought in specialists from the Moran Eye Center. Because this reaction (also called "Stevens Johnsons Syndrome)" is known to damage the eyes, they brought in medical students to become acquainted with its effects. They tried different lenses, but because of the damage to her eye, nothing helped. They explained that down-the-road, they would need to have a cornea transplant.

After we were home, Dr. Mortensen, our own optometrist, checked her eyes. He came to the house on a regular basis to remove eyelashes which were growing in "wild" and scratching the surface of her eye. To solve this problem, some months later we took Julene to Salt Lake City, where Dr. Branson Call performed eyelid surgery to remove these eyelashes that were damaging her eyes. These lashes had caused pain and were destructive to her cornea. The surgery was successful and her eyes seemed better.

On Saturday, January 2, 1999, Julene awoke to excruciating pain in the area of her sinuses. We called Dr. Grant Davis, ENT, who came to our house and reported that not much appeared to be wrong, and suggested we call our eye doctor. Dr. Mortensen came, opened the eyelid, and found that her cornea was extremely thin.

Immediately, we called our Salt Lake doctor, who soon informed us there was not a cornea available. However, he wanted us to bring Julene to Salt Lake where she was again admitted to LDS Hospital. On Monday night, a cornea became available. On Tuesday morning, the cornea specialist came to Julene's hospital room to talk to us. He said: "If this is a match, you better take it, even if you aren't feeling well. If your cornea ruptures, you will lose your eye in 48 hours." He then looked at her eye. He seemed concerned but didn't say much more. However, he came back an hour later with a portable microscope and announced, "Your cornea has already ruptured. Let's hope this is a good match."

Terry and I had been fasting. We had been listening to tapes on why we suffer while here on earth. And Julene was suffering—beyond the usual suffering caused by the damage to her lungs. We called Elder Dellenbach, the member of the Quorum of the Seventy who had been "watching over" Julene since the second week of her hospitalization. He came shortly before Julene was taken into surgery. With great power, he again blessed her.

The cornea was tested and it was a good match. The doctors took Julene into surgery as soon as the normally scheduled patients were finished, which was about six p.m. They suggested the procedure would last about two hours. But instead, it lasted four hours. When they finally brought Julene out of surgery, a pair of very tired doctors said they had saved her eye. They explained that before they could sew the new cornea in place, they had first reconstructed the eye. That took a very long time.

What a miracle! A matching cornea had appeared just when her cornea ruptured. Doctors had the skill to reconstruct her eye. Yet this miracle was at an enormous cost in terms of pain and suffering. The last time Julene had been in surgery, her breathing was so compromised afterward, that she almost died. A hospital pharmacist had narrowed it down to a reaction to the morphine used for pain control. So, because of the high risk of using morphine, Julene was only given a large dose of Motrin (Ibuprofen) to control the horrendous pain after eye surgery. In all her suffering, Julene said this was the most intense, terrible pain she had experienced. And it lasted several hours. The whole night was spent trying to comfort her and help her sleep, even a little.

We were so thankful for this cornea transplant, even though it had been so agonizingly difficult. Although it allowed her to keep her eye, her vision was still somewhat cloudy and became worse. Two other miracles that eventually allowed her to see are described later in this chapter.

"And Jesus answered and said unto him, What wilt thou that I should do unto thee? The blind man said unto him, Lord, that I might receive my sight" (Mark 20:51).

MIRACLE #20
THE MIRACLES OF "HIS" WATCHFUL CARE.

In our pre-mortal life, we fought to have the gift of agency. Agency allows us to make choices, but it does not remove Heavenly Father's role in watching over us and helping us. Nevertheless, as we go about our busy lives, we are often unaware how much the Lord supports and blesses us in our times of need.

With Julene's long-term suffering, we were aware on a daily basis that the Lord was watching over her and us. Nevertheless, there were two occasions that we knew without a doubt that He was aware of the most minute details of her life.

The same eye that had received the cornea transplant began to hurt. One morning at 4 a.m. she had a terrible pain in that eye. Dr. Mortensen again came to the house and confirmed that there was a serious problem. She needed another cornea transplant. We headed to Salt Lake, hoping a cornea would be found. This time, a young person's cornea was available, so they were hoping this one would last better than her first transplant. As they prepared for the eye surgery, they were able to measure the thickness of the existing cornea; it was only <u>one cell thick.</u> One of the medical students present for the transplant came out and told us that he knew he had just experienced a miracle. Julene's extremely thin cornea had remained intact until they were able to give her the new cornea. The Lord had truly preserved her eye again.

The second situation that showed God's watchful care was regarding her oxygen supply. Most of us rarely think about our oxygen and how necessary it is for all life. Julene's need for oxygen was paramount in every moment and every situation both in a hospital and while she was home.

Julene's blood oxygen dropped below safe levels frequently, and it became our responsibility to monitor this and provide the proper amounts of oxygen. A huge tank of oxygen was placed in the garage, and there was a tube running through the house to wherever Julene was. We had smaller tanks she used if she needed to be transported.

Each time we drove to Salt Lake for a medical procedure, we took two or three tanks of oxygen with us. In March of 2000, we had been in Salt Lake for a series of medical procedures and were headed home. Usually, we stopped at a truck-stop so Julene could use the restroom. However, on this particular trip, Julene decided she did not need to stop. It was always difficult to get her out of the car, help her walk through the convenience store dragging an oxygen tank, and help her in the restroom. And washing her hands was even frustrating because the soap immediately caused a rash on her hands. So, we drove straight home. We had considered trading to the second tank of oxygen, because we were running low, but decided we could get home without the change.

Rick Smith, one of the respiratory therapists whose company provided the oxygen, met us at our house with a newly-filled huge tank of oxygen. As we got Julene into the house, he immediately changed to the tank in the garage. He looked at the small tank and said: "The tank she was using is <u>completely empty</u>!" Looking at the alternate tank (which had been traded at the hospital when we left), he continued: "And the valve on this tank is wrong—you could not have used it." Again, we knew the Lord had watched over Julene, because within a very few minutes on room air, Julene would have been unconscious and would have suffered brain damage.

"Are not five sparrows sold for two farthings, and not one of them is forgotten before God? But even the very hairs of your head are all numbered. Fear not therefore: ye are of more value than many sparrows" (Luke 12: 6-7).

TRIALS CONTINUED

The spring of 2000 continued to be difficult for Julene and for our family—and probably for some of neighbors who continued to support us over this long trial. This time period has become a blur in my memory because I was so exhausted. I started eating chocolate bars about 1 a.m. to have enough energy to finish the details of helping Julene be ready to sleep. One night, I lay on the floor next to her bed telling Julene I just needed to rest for a minute or two. She patiently waited 20 minutes and then made a loud noise with a squeaky toy—my signal that she needed me.

With such fatigue, I am not surprised that I did not remember all the difficulties we experienced during these months. Julene shared the details of the trials in a letter she wrote to her high school friend, Nick Munns, who was serving a mission in Norway. This is presented in its entirety with only minor corrections:

Dear Nick,

I'm sorry that it always takes me so long to write back. I guess I'm not a very good pen pal. It's always so much fun to get your letters. The last one was a treat because you responded to almost everything I mentioned. In fact, sometimes I couldn't remember exactly what I had told you. :-)

NEWS UPDATE! Carla is engaged! Of course, that's probably not really a surprise, but in a way, it is. I mean Carla, my little sister, is getting married! Crazy, huh? She is no longer going to be coming to Norway. Apparently, BYU didn't want to pay for a group to travel all the way to Europe just to do one concert. But that works out better for the wedding plans. So, they aren't too upset!

I'm afraid this letter is going to sound like it's all about Carla, but... A week and a half ago, I had yet another eye surgery. This one was an amniotic membrane/stem cell transplant. They removed the scar tissues from the surface of my eye and replaced it with the amniotic tissue. Then they took some tissue from Carla's eye (she was a perfect match!) and grafted that to my eye also. The cells they took from Carla is a special type that helps your own cells regenerate and repair themselves. If this surgery works, my cornea transplant will last longer because my eye will be able to heal itself and regenerate the new surface tissue to protect the cornea. It really is miraculous what they can do now days!

You asked me to tell you about some spiritual experiences that I have had. Approaching this last surgery, I had a lot of somewhat difficult decisions to make. My lungs had really not been doing well and I have had to take some medicines that are great while you can take them, but cannot be used indefinitely. To ask Carla to jeopardize her eye by giving me 70 percent of her stem cell tissue seemed like something really hard to ask, should I become sick enough that I cannot enjoy the eyesight. Unless something happened, we considered delaying the surgery.

Truman Madsen, a well-known author & lecturer from BYU, was speaking at Devotional at Ricks College and came over to meet me and visit with me before the Devotional. He suggested that being included on the First Presidency prayer roll and having a large group of people fast for a purpose were two very effective ways of getting answers to questions or prayers. Sister Madsen called Elder Scott and ask him to include my name on the prayer roll, which is the first Thursday of every month. We asked our Bishop if the ward could fast on Fast Sunday. We also invited friends and my family to participate.

My friend from the General Relief Society Board, Sister King, and her husband drove up from Utah to spend the weekend and join our fast. Then suddenly everything seemed to go wrong. My feeding tube burst out of my stomach, making it very difficult to feed me because the contents of my stomach would not stay in. (Sorry this is kind of gross!) We made temporary repairs as best we could, but it was difficult to get the nourishment I needed to keep my lungs healthy before the surgery. In the March Ensign, there was an article by Jeffrey R. Holland that explains that there is often adversity before or after a great spiritual experience. Surely that must have been what was happening. President King and my Dad gave me a blessing. As we made arrangements to take [care of] our problems,

Sister Olivia King and Julene

amazingly everyone we needed to contact was on call and on hospital duty for the period of time I would need their help. I was admitted to LDS Hospital on Monday and things were taken care of so that I was rested and was ready for the surgery on Wednesday at a different hospital. I really believe that the help was available when I needed it, and I was blessed in many other ways because of the faith and prayers of so many people. I know that Heavenly Father loves me and is aware of my suffering. I am thankful for the small miracles and blessings that I always receive. Your family were among the friends that fasted for me.

MIRACLE #21
THE MIRACLE OF REVELATION AND AN APOSTLE'S VISIT

Throughout Julene's trial, we often felt we were guided by inspiration. But there were at least two occasions where we felt there was true revelation. One was directly to me, and the other was to someone else but for Julene and us.

In July, 1999, the Ricks College Folk Dancers and Bluegrass Band were giving their performance prior to a month-long tour to Europe. I was in charge of the band and needed to attend. Terry came home from the farm to stay with Julene. When I arrived home about two hours later, I got ready to give her the third dose of medicine from an inhaler. With the inhaler in hand, I approached Julene. I then heard a voice say: "Don't give her that medicine. It is hurting her." I thought back about the two doses earlier in the day and realized that she had had a very difficult time immediately after I administered the medicine to her. The next day I shared this experience with her pulmonologist, Dr. Nathan Dean, in Salt Lake. He said that it was unusual to have a reaction to that medicine, but with Julene, it was definitely a possibility. So, with his permission, we discontinued the use of the inhaler.

It was Monday, March 7, 2000, when we took Julene to Salt Lake to have the feeding tube in her abdomen relocated because of the leakage. On Tuesday, she had some routine respiratory tests done. As she was to be at LDS Hospital overnight, her pulmonologist, Dr. Dean, said he was running late and asked if he could keep an appointment at his office with a general authority and come back later to give her the results of the afternoon tests. Understanding how busy general authorities are, she readily agreed.

When Dr. Dean returned, he told her that the good news was that her lungs had actually improved. The sad news was that the trachea had become less healthy. She had tracheomalacia, which meant the trachea was collapsing, making it especially difficult to exhale. He told us that she would slowly get worse. It would become so difficult to breathe that she would be put on morphine, and eventually she would suffocate.

It was at this time we recognized the blessing of a second revelation. Dr. Dean's appointment was with Elder Robert D. Hales, who was having respiratory distress and was on supplemental oxygen. He told Elder Hales about Julene and explained what had happened to her. Elder Hales felt impressed that he needed to visit Julene, and he asked for directions to her hospital room. With difficulty, Elder Hales and his wife Mary came to Julene's hospital room. They talked with her and asked if there was anything he could do for her. Julene asked if he would give her a blessing. He said he would be honored to do so. When he blessed her, he assured her that the Lord loved her. Toward the end, he stated: "If it is the Lord's will that you continue to live on the earth, you will get well. If it is the Lord's will that you return to Him, you will return to Him."

We were all blessed by both his presence and the words of his blessing. We knew it was through the miracle of revelation that Elder Hales came to bless Julene and assure her that the Lord still loved her and watched over her.

Julene's appointment on Wednesday was with Dr. Mark Mifflin, for the surgery to give her the new amniotic membrane so her eye would continue to regenerate properly. After her recovery that afternoon, we took Julene home once again.

A few days after being home, we received a beautiful letter addressed to Terry and me from Elder Hales. He thanked us for allowing him to give our beautiful daughter a blessing. He said he felt a beautiful spirit of purity and sweetness that flowed from Julene. He reaffirmed the love that Heavenly Father had for Julene.

Julene wrote a thank you note to Elder Hales. She included some photographs in her letter.

During the month that she was home, her health continued to decline. On April 26, 2000, she said she was just so tired that she didn't want to get out of bed. To give her as much rest as possible, I left her on the ventilator. About 11 a.m. I brought in the mail, and was surprised to see a second letter from Elder Hales. I read Julene his touching letter in which he expressed his hope that she was improving and that she would feel love and comfort from the Savior. He added a handwritten note mentioning the need for faith and patience. He ended with: "Our thoughts and prayers are with you always."

I set the letter down and turned to see that blood had filled her ventilator tubes. I tried to suction, but the blood kept coming; she was experiencing massive hemorrhaging from her trachea. She looked at the tubing and said: "Mom, look—there is blood in the tubes." I told her: "I know, and I have been suctioning, but it isn't coming out." Unsure of what else to do, I leaned over and said, "I love you." She looked at me and answered with a phrase she had used so many times, "I love you more." Unable to receive air, her eyes closed and she passed on quietly—from this time of terrible suffering into the arms of our Savior, where death and sorrow are known no more.

"If thou shalt ask, thou shalt receive revelation upon revelation, knowledge upon knowledge"

(D&C 42:61).

BOOK III

THE IMPACT OF ONE ANGEL

CHAPTER ELEVEN
JULENE'S SUFFERING STIRRED MANY HEARTS

As soon as our friends and neighbors heard of Julene's catastrophic and life-threatening condition, there were many prayers offered in her behalf. Children who didn't even know Julene began praying for her morning and night. Members of the LDS Church also pray for those with special needs by putting a person's name on the prayer rolls in our temples. Because many members contacted their friends or relatives in many different temple districts, Julene's name was entered in temple prayer rolls all across the country, and possibly the world.

Sister Olivia King, in her funeral address, shared this comment:

> When many are praying on behalf of someone in need, then when prayers are answered and the suffering is relieved, all have shared together in the pain, and all partake of the comfort. When many people have worked for the sufferer's relief, then all kneel together and give thanks to the Lord, then the suffering has served the vital purpose of drawing many different people together and making them brothers and sisters. (See Chapter 13)

As time passed, and Julene was still hospitalized but awake, many sent cards and letters. A dear friend and neighbor gave colorful note paper to many of the children in our neighborhood as well as to several adults and asked them to write messages of encouragement. One young boy wrote on the belly of a green dragon: "Dear Julene, I think that you will get better because we all pray and hope for [you]. Love, Dallin"

A young man, probably high school age, wrote on a sunflower page: "Dear Julene, You don't know me but I'm sure you're a great person. We've been fasting and praying for you and you're continually in our prayers and thoughts. Sincerely, Hyrum."

Children who were too young to write, drew pictures; some attached school pictures with "Get Well Soon" and printed their name.

One ten-year-old girl, who also sent her message on a sunflower, was very practical and tried to cheer Julene. "Hi! Get Well Soon. My room is decorated in sunflowers and now yours can be to! Miss you bunches! Heidi"

A dear friend of many years added her thoughts again on a sunflower page that said:

Dear Julene, Many people have shown their love for you through prayers and fasting over the past months. There has been a great outpouring of love that can't be seen--but hopefully you have felt or have been told about by your dear parents. No one but the Lord may know of the total numbers who care about you and your recovery. Know that you are loved by sooo many!

Love, Marybeth Jones." [Her husband, Brent Jones, wrote an arrangement of hymns for violin and cello for Julene's funeral.]

An older sister in our neighborhood and ward who was an artist, a writer and journalist by profession, wrote a poem to our family to convey her thoughts:

Friends are a priceless gift that can't be bought or sold.
Their value is far greater than mountains made of gold.
For gold is cold and lifeless, nor can it see or hear,
And in troubled times, it has no heart to give us cheer
So, when you pray for comfort, be thankful God sends
Not diamonds, pearls and riches, but the love of true and faithful friends.

For with friends we are never alone or forsaken in illness and despair.
God gives us help and guidance, friends give loving comfort and care.
Given all the friends who love you, you have a miracle gift called love
To inspire and strengthen your family, it comes from Heaven above.
May God bless and hearten your hopes and belief,
An abiding hope for courageous Julene's relief
Is the prayer of a friend who marvels at such family harmony.
So, sing with praise, sing with hope and unity of thankful hearts.
May your voices ring with gratitude for such a creative, devoted family.

God bless you all,

A grateful friend, Ellen Genta

Julene received a very special letter from a lady she did not know. Brenda Benedict, from Kooskia, Idaho, had heard about Julene from her nephew, Jared Benedict—the good-looking one! She wrote it in big letters, undoubtedly hoping Julene could read it herself. She also ordered a pizza to be delivered!

Dear Juleen,

Your story has blessed our lives! (and made us cry)... I feel like we are living near a modern-day JOB family. You are amazing. You have been through so much... and yet you still have courage and faith. You have taught us so much. I am writing to say two things.

#1: I want to say thank you to you and to your family for what you have given to ours. Your parents must be incredible. I hope to have a valiant spirit like they must have... like you have. I'm sure many days are more difficult than anyone can imagine... yet you are doing it. Jared says you guys are wonderful.

#2: I want to tell you that our family is praying for you and thinking about you. Even though we've not met, we care so much. I will fast each Tues. that you will be healed and that you all are given extra strength. I wish I could do more... even share some of your pain. In more ways than my heart can hold I want you to know that you are loved. I'm enclosing a hug. sincerely & with love, (and another for your mom)... Brenda Benedict

WILL KEEP COMING ... + JUST KEEP COMING ...!

92

Jared, who spent the summer of 1999 in California and was no longer able to visit, wrote to Julene each Sunday afternoon. In this letter he wrote telling Julene how much she had influenced him.

Julene,

I loved your letter . . . You seriously have a gift for looking beyond your trials and keeping your sense of humor. That not only takes a lot of strength, but a great depth as well. I think that's why I am so driven to keep in touch with you, so that I can let some of your depth rub off on me.

By the way, have I ever gone off on what a wonderful friend you've been to me over the years? I mean other than the fact that you have to listen to me no matter whether you like it or not when I come over. J/K.

Seriously, I don't know just how to put it into words, but I'm a better person because I've known you. You have no idea how much I enjoyed being able to spend Sundays with you and your family. I believe I've told you this before, but there is a reassurance that comes from long-time friends. It's kind of like an anchor in an ever-changing world. What I'm trying to say is regardless of what happens between now and forever, we're always going to be best friends, and even though that may sound dumb, it still means a lot to me.

Love, Jared Max (Benedict)

Perhaps the comment of the former LDS branch president, who served at the University of Utah Hospital, tells how Julene had an impact on total strangers. About a year and a half after Julene left the burn center, we saw this good brother and visited with him in the entrance of LDS Hospital when Julene was there as an out-patient. He commented: "People who just saw her in the hall or in her room would go their way and be thankful for their own problems."

We will never know how far Julene's influence spread during the two and a half years she battled for her life. We do know that her story spread far and wide. One day, our daughter Margo was at the apartment of a friend in Provo. Her friend's cousin was visiting from Michigan and told the sad story of a girl who had had a terrible reaction to penicillin. After listening for a while, Margo said: "That's my sister."

93

CHAPTER TWELVE
AT JULENE'S PASSING

The outpouring of love that followed Julene's passing surpassed anything we could have imagined. After being so totally involved with her care, we did not realize how many of our friends, neighbors, teachers, business associates, as well as the medical community had been so deeply touched by Julene's struggle to live. As might be expected, we knew flowers would be sent. However, the number of flower arrangements and living plants that we received was indeed astounding.

Our mailbox was filled with cards and letters, telling us how much the sender had been touched by Julene's faith and courage. I was truly surprised that doctors would take time to send condolences—some even handwritten. Here are the messages from two doctors who cared for Julene:

Dear Folks,

I appreciated your call about Julene, and I was saddened to hear that she had passed away. I was very impressed by her courage and stamina, which, despite overwhelming odds, allowed her intellect and wit to show through. I remember fondly our dinner where we played the game that allowed her to shine. I still play the (Bluegrass) tape that you gave me of your family band, and I can't help but feel that you will be together playing again in some better place at some future day. I am sure that Julene has found peace and is just waiting to see you again.

I have very much enjoyed knowing you and admire your courage and devotion.

Best Regards, N. Branson Call, M.D.
(the eye doctor who had fasted for Julene, surgically removed her wild eyelashes, and had dinner at our house with Julene)

* * * * * *

Dear Wilcox Family,

I want you to know what a great privilege it was to participate in the care of Julene. I will always remember her and I know that her valiant spirit lives on. She (and you all) have been an excellent example of love, service, and enduring to the end. Please let me know if there is anything I can do for you.

Sincerely, Mark Mifflin, M.D.
(the eye surgeon who restored Julene's vision)

* * * * * *

It had been two years since Julene had been discharged from the burn center, but they sent a beautiful card signed by many of the nurses and therapists who had attended Julene. That medical unit sees so many patients with difficult, heart-wrenching conditions that I was surprised that this nurse wrote: "I am so sad to hear about Julene. She (and you) touched many lives here. She worked so hard to heal. Julene was a beautiful and very brave young woman. We will never forget her. My thoughts and prayers are with you." Many others wrote short messages that expressed how Julene was "a very special person," or "a sweetheart." Some wrote that they were thankful to have been part of our lives. One said: "I'm sorry—but she's singing her best now!"

* * * * * *

The Relief Society General Presidency sent a beautiful message:

Dear Brother and Sister Wilcox and Family:

We express sincere condolences at the passing of your daughter and sister and pray your hearts will be filled with peace and that you will find comfort in your understanding of the gospel.

Julene's love for life and positive attitude were an inspiration to all who came in contact with her.

We pray that Heavenly Father will help make us equal that we may return to meet again with Julene and watch her progression through eternity.

With sincere sympathy, Relief Society General Presidency
Mary Ellen Smoot, Virginia U. Jensen, Sheri L. Dew

* * * * * *

One of our neighbors, a former home teacher, sent a beautiful card and this heart-warming message:

Terry and Eileen,

Linda and I want to express to you our sympathy. You and your family have always been such a good example to us. When I was your home teacher, I loved to visit your home and hear from you and your girls. Your girls are so beautiful inside and out. The etching on the front of Julene's program was a great illustration of her relationship with the Savior. I know God doesn't take a righteous person from the earth until they have finished their mission. Julene served so faithfully and touched many lives even during her suffering. Those events at the end of her mission have prepared her for service in God's Spiritual Kingdom. The memories of Julene will continue to bless our lives and the knowledge of God's plan keeps us close to her and others no longer in our presence. Our thoughts and prayers are with you. Know of our love, and we thank you for your goodness.

Rick, Linda Merrill & Boys

* * * * * *

Several of the families of my music students sent flowers and notes telling us of the memories they had of Julene at a younger age:

Dear Eileen, Terry, & family,

We extend our love and deepest sympathy. I remember Julene as such a beautiful talented girl with those laughing, sparkling eyes. I'm sure you'll find great comfort in the happy times you've had as a family and in the gospel. Our prayers are with you still.

Randy & Susan Brown and family

* * * * * *

Many have wondered and a few have asked what feelings our immediate family had. Although we were broken-hearted to let Julene leave us, we were so grateful that her terrible suffering had ended. One cannot imagine the indescribable fear that came upon her every time her breathing was compromised, and that was a near daily occurrence. We rejoiced that she no longer was hooked up to a ventilator and tied to a source of oxygen! But her room seemed so very, very empty.

Audra, her youngest sister, was a little over four and a half years old when Julene died. She was very quick to say: "Now Mommy, maybe now you will have time for me!" And before the funeral directors had left, Anneli, who was 10 years old, asked if she could move into Julene's bedroom and paint it lavender. Neither probably remembered much of what our home was like before Julene was ill.

Undoubtedly, the older girls were the most devastated emotionally, because they were so close in age and had done so many things together, especially performing and touring together. Margo had married four months prior to Julene's passing. Carla was engaged and had planned her wedding reception to be held in our yard so Julene could be present without having to leave home. Consequently, the four weeks following Julene's death turned into a flurry of sewing bridesmaid dresses, planting flowers and doing other yardwork, and making the house presentable. I'm sure working toward this happy event helped us all to move forward.

CHAPTER THIRTEEN
JULENE'S FUNERAL

Julene's funeral was held on May 1, 2000, at 2 p.m. at the Rexburg 12th Ward chapel. The day was beautiful and sunny. The chapel and the cultural hall were both filled to capacity.

Because Julene and our family were so involved with music, the musical numbers were meaningful as well as beautiful. One of her teachers at Ricks College, Brent Jones, wrote a violin and cello arrangement of "Nearer My God to Thee" and "I Am a Child of God." It was played by her sisters SaraLyn and Carla, and accompanied by Brother Jones. After the life sketch given by my brother, Keith Wilhoit, and a meaningful talk by our faithful home teacher, Shane Goodwin, Julene's voice teacher, Florence Bowman sang: "The Lamb" by K. Newell Dayley. This was the piece Julene sang as a solo for the Ricks College Devotional the summer of 1996.

Next, Sister Olivia King of the Relief Society general board spoke and first related how she learned about Julene and her sad plight. She then related what a special relationship she had with our daughter. She said that her heart was forever changed just from meeting Julene. She felt like they were truly sisters, just that "one came earlier, and one came later."

Sister King introduced her friend, Sister Jean Keaton, the artist who made the beautiful drawing that was printed on the front of the funeral program and which is reproduced at the end of this chapter. Sister King had commissioned the work—an 11" x 14" drawing and had it beautifully framed. She had presented this to Julene earlier in the year. She wanted it to show how beautiful Julene was; and how, throughout this trial, the Savior was right by her side. She noted that when looking at the drawing, you could see the imprint of the nail in His hand, and reminded us that He also went through much struggling and pain.

One time, while visiting our daughter, Sister King had asked Julene to share her favorite scripture with her. Found in D&C 6:34 and 36, it says:

"Therefore, fear not, little flock; do good; let earth and hell combine against you, for if ye are built upon my rock, they cannot prevail.

"Look unto me in every thought; doubt not, fear not."

Sister Keaton included the last part of this scripture on the drawing of Julene with Christ.

During these two years, Sister King had become close to Julene and our family. She sought for answers in the scriptures that would give comfort and encouragement to Julene, our family, and to others who were aware of Julene. She then read the scriptures that she had shared to encourage Julene.

Alma 36:3: "For I do know that whosoever shall put their trust in God shall be supported in their trials, and their troubles, and their afflictions, and shall be lifted up at the last day."

Matthew 28:20: "Lo, I am with you alway, even unto the ends of the world. Amen."

D&C 88:63: "Draw near unto me and I will draw near unto you."

D&C 84:88: "For I will go before your face. I will be on your right hand and on your left, and my Spirit shall be in your hearts, and mine angels round about you, to bear you up.

Sister King went beyond the scriptures and found statements from an earlier prophet, Joseph F. Smith, who testified that the spirit and the body will be reunited; and from Orson F. Whitney, who said that our pain, suffering and trials help develop our character and purify our hearts.

Over several months, Sister King had witnessed how much love, sacrifice and devotion we as Julene's parents continued to provide. She wanted to do something for Julene that she felt we could not do. On October 27, 1998—one year after the reaction and before one of Julene's surgeries, she asked us to leave Julene's room for a little while. She said: "With a pen and paper in my hand, and my ear close to her mouth, she dictated this letter to her parents." Sister King had given us a beautiful copy of this letter shortly after Julene had dictated it. However, she shared it at the funeral to show Julene's gratitude, sweetness, love and humility in the midst of her continued suffering.

Dear Mom and Dad,

I want to take this opportunity to thank you for the love, time and support that you've given me. It's been so choice that you would spend so much time with me. I feel like I've come to know you like I never would have, if I hadn't got sick.

Dad,

You are a spiritual giant, and I love it! I love the way we study the scriptures together. I even like the Tabernacle Choir CD's you brought in. Thank you for staying up with me when I can't go to sleep. For skipping meals so that you could be with me. Thank you for taking so much time off of work for me. Thank you for including me in the campus ward special fast.
I LOVE YOU . . .more

Mom,

Thanks for letting me be a mama's girl. You've always been there when I wanted to cry on someone's shoulder. Thank you for your persistence in trying to find ways to help me. It helps me to believe that I will get better. Because I knew that you will never give up! Thank you for sharing your time that you could be spending with my little sisters Anneli and Audra.
I LOVE YOU . . .lots

I know that this year has been very hard on all of you. I know that it is hard to have a relationship when you only see each other once a week. I admire you.
I LOVE YOU . . .lots more

Julene

To me, one of the sweetest thing Sister King shared was this: "I testify to you that every time I walked into Julene's room, I felt that I was in the presence of angels, and one of the sweetest angels laid in that bed.

Sister King said in conclusion: "My life will forever be changed because of Julene."

We were so pleased when Elder Robert K. Dellenbach accepted the invitation to speak at Julene's funeral. He had visited her, blessed her, and rejoiced with her as she had made small steps of recovery. His address was a powerful testimony of our Savior, Jesus Christ, and Julene's relationship to Him, and it gave us a great measure of comfort.

Like Sister King, Elder Dellenbach explained how when he first met Julene, he was fulfilling a responsibility—a request to go to the Burn Center at the University Hospital to bless a young girl in need. Then he described the condition Julene was in when he first saw her. "Her body was one complete mass of pus and bleeding flesh, her features almost indistinguishable. I've never seen anyone in such total hurt as she was." He said he wondered if she could possibly live— because there was nothing left of her. Yet he said he distinctly remembered blessing her that if it were the Lord's will, that she would continue to live. He noted that for two and a half years, she courageously fought to stay alive. But he felt that now the Lord's will "that she not continue on," and he quoted Job 1:21: "The Lord gave, and the Lord hath taken away; blessed be the name of the Lord."

Although I don't remember that Elder Dellenbach had ever had the opportunity to see or hear Julene playing her banjo, he was aware that she had been on tour with performance groups with both BYU and Ricks College. He had traveled with these groups and knew how the performers lifted those in the audience, both on stage and afterwards as they mingled with the audience. He felt that Julene had been "called home" to perhaps continue performing in an even greater calling than she had had on earth. Later in his talk he suggested she might be

101

playing her heavenly banjo, as well as singing and dancing. In this way she would be bearing testimony of Jesus Christ.

Elder Dellenbach reminded us of the miracle of Lazarus as found in John, chapter 11, and particularly verse 26 when Jesus said: "I am the resurrection, and the life: he that believeth in me, though he were dead, yet shall he live. And [he that] liveth and believeth in me shall never die."

He then quoted a portion of the 138th Section of the Doctrine and Covenants, so we would more fully understand the spirit world and the place where Julene was. This section is a vision President Joseph F. Smith had two months before his death as he was pondering on the scriptures:

"These the Lord taught, and gave them power to come forth, after his resurrection from the dead, to enter into his Father's kingdom, there to be crowned with immortality and eternal life,

"And continue thenceforth their labor as had been promised by the Lord, and be partakers of all blessings which were held in reserve for them that love him.

"The Prophet Joseph Smith, and my father, Hyrum Smith, Brigham Young, John Taylor, Wilford Woodruff, and other choice spirits who were reserved to come forth in the fulness of times to take part in laying the foundations of the great latter-day work,

"Including the building of the temples and the performance of ordinances therein for the redemption of the dead, were also in the spirit world.

"I observed that they were also among the noble and great ones who were chosen in the beginning to be rulers in the Church of God.

"Even before they were born, they, with many others, received their first lessons in the world of spirits and were prepared to come forth in the due time of the Lord to labor in his vineyard for the salvation of the souls of men.

"I beheld that the faithful elders of this dispensation, when they depart from mortal life, continue their labors in the preaching of the gospel of repentance and redemption, through the sacrifice of the

102

Only Begotten Son of God, among those who are in darkness and under the bondage of sin in the great world of the spirits of the dead" (D&C 138:51-57).

Elder Dellenbach assured us Julene would be sharing her testimony and preaching the gospel in the spirit world. He helped us understand the glory of the Father's kingdom so we wouldn't be so sad at Julene's departure from us.

As he concluded his address, he shared his testimony and witness of the Savior Jesus Christ and the reality of His atoning sacrifice. He expressed his gratitude for the opportunity he had had to know Julene, to love her, and to feel her presence. He said: "Thank God for Julene Wilcox!"

Following Elder Dellenbach's testimony, the closing song was "I Believe in Christ." It was played as a string quartet by our four girls in an arrangement I had written, and one that we had performed many times with Julene. The congregation joined us, singing verses 3 and 4.

Casket and flowers for
Julene Vivian Wilcox

Julene was buried at Annis Little Butte Cemetery next to her baby brother, Cory Keith Wilcox, who died when he was only one year old. He died from complications of a genetic defect in 1984. How wonderful they can be together!

Look unto me in
every thought;
doubt not, fear not.
D&C 6:36

105

CHAPTER FOURTEEN
SUFFERING AND OUR SAVIOR

In Elder Bruce R. McConkie's book, <u>All These Things Shall Give Thee Experience</u>, he lists three reasons why we suffer in mortality. The first is because of sin and our own poor choices. The second is because of the natural causes of disease, aging, and accidents. The third reason is to give us the experience necessary to be worthy to attain Godhood and eternal life. This type of suffering comes to righteous, worthy individuals who are able to continue their earthly refinement through what may appear to be "unfair" situations or conditions.

When Elder Dellenbach visited Julene the very first time, he recounted that he had also visited and blessed two young men who were hospitalized and in critical condition. He said they had been driving a motorcycle and had been going much too fast on mountain roads with unfavorable road conditions. He felt compassion for their condition, but pointed out that their suffering was the result of their lack of respect for life itself. Then he said: "But Julene is suffering through no fault of her own. She has done nothing to bring on this terrible condition." He commented that too many times we as mortals do not respect the sanctity of life, and we are not wise in our choices.

Many have criticized the decisions of the Martin and Willey handcart companies to leave so late in the year. Yet, they recorded that they were blessed in their afflictions. President Faust recounted the story in his Conference talk of 1979, and is here quoted only in part:

"We suffered beyond anything you can imagine and many died of exposure and starvation, but did you ever hear a survivor of that company utter a word of criticism? Not one of that company ever apostatized or left the Church, because everyone of us came through with the absolute knowledge that God lives for we became acquainted with him in our extremities.

"'Was I sorry that I chose to come by handcart? No. Neither then nor any minute of my life since. The price we paid to become acquainted with God was a privilege to pay, and I am thankful that I was privileged to come in the Martin Handcart Company'" (David O. McKay, "Pioneer Women," *Relief Society Magazine,* Jan. 1948, 8).

Then President Faust added: "Here then is a great truth. In the pain, the agony, and the heroic endeavors of life, we pass through a refiner's fire, and the insignificant and the unimportant in our lives can melt away like dross and make our faith bright, intact, and strong. In this way the divine image can be mirrored from the soul. It is part of the purging toll exacted of some to become acquainted with God. In the agonies of life, we seem to listen better to the faint, godly whisperings of the Divine Shepherd" (James E. Faust, "The Refiner's Fire," Ensign, May 1979, 53)

As we have sorted through Julene's papers and journals, we found that she kept notes about the scriptures she read, and she wrote reports on the Conference talks she studied. She was very concerned about living righteously and being a witness for Christ.

Although Julene's prolonged affliction may appear to be the result of natural causes, such as disease, it seems that Julene's suffering was for her refinement and perhaps for that of her family and others. We are told that Abraham was asked to sacrifice his only son, Isaac to understand God's allowing His only son to be sacrificed for the good of all mankind. Julene's afflictions mirrored the pain that Christ suffered. We know that Jesus bled from every pore; and when Julene had skin loss from 65 percent of her body, she bled in a similar fashion. When we study the cause of death in crucifixion, we learn that the person actually suffocates in a slow and agonizing manner. Julene's breathing also became compromised to the point that she was suffocating. But through the compassion of our Savior, she was able to die quickly when suddenly blood filled her bronchial tubes and then her lungs.

Julene's suffering, in turn, caused us to become closer to God and be more aware of our need to be pure and consecrated. At one point in Julene's recovery, we set up a television in her room, and her sister brought home a DVD of a recent comedy for her to watch. After watching for about thirty minutes, Julene asked why we were watching this movie. When we questioned what was wrong, Julene said: "In the first place, it pictures a man and a woman living in the same apartment without being married." Then she listed other inappropriate situations. Even though there were no visual displays of vice, Julene was offended with the ideas of immorality and deception portrayed on the screen. She was living so close to the Spirit, that she could not enjoy the vices Satan portrays as acceptable.

Our faith, as well as Julene's, was developed as we prayed for miracles and received them. We were aware that there were those who questioned this trial, especially when it ended in death. Those who truly understood the refinement that comes through pain and suffering and believed in God's plan and purpose for mortal life, came away with a stronger testimony of our Savior and His atoning sacrifice.

We, as a family, KNOW that Julene is not dead, but lives still. We, as well as others, have been given this sure knowledge. Wondering if we would remember this touching event, Dr. Mark Mifflin recently reminded us in an email about a dream he had shortly after Julene's death:

> Dear Terry and Eileen,
>
> On a tender mercy note, I don't know if you remember me calling shortly after Julene died. I was prompted to call you because I had had a dream about Julene.
>
> I think that I spoke only briefly with Eileen, and she informed me that Julene had passed. I don't think I told you specifics about the dream at the time, but I am a vivid and frequent dreamer and often remember my dreams. I had not seen Julene for quite some time, and did not know that there was an acute situation with her health. This was a very short and particularly vivid dream in terms of visual detail. Julene was standing, talking, seeing, and most of all smiling. But she still had a little sadness in her face. She looked healthy. (I never saw her look healthy in mortality.) I could see her eyes well, and they were both clear and normal-looking, even sparkling, perhaps with a little tearing. She thanked me for helping her with her eyes. I don't remember the exact words but the interaction was brief and it seemed like there were audible words, not just thoughts. After several seconds she

was gone. I don't think I awoke immediately, but was a little shaken by the memory of the dream. I fell back into my usual busy routine, but was still wondering about the significance of the experience. After a few days I called and discovered she had died.

I have actually had this experience with one other former patient as well (in 25 years) so I don't think it was random or coincidental. I have shared my experience about her appearance in my dream with only trusted friends and family as I consider it a sacred experience.

(personal email from Dr. Mifflin; shared with permission).

On more than one occasion, we have felt Julene's presence. Her sister, Margo, shared this beautiful and sacred story in a sacrament meeting when she was asked to speak about temples:

One of the most special temple experiences I have had, happened shortly after Dan and I were married. My sister, Julene, who was my best friend and roommate, died not long after we had been married. We had been moved to Kentucky to work on a job there. And for a while, there wasn't a temple near us since the Louisville temple was not yet finished. When the Louisville temple was completed we went to the temple. I think it was only my second or third time attending the temple and I was a little nervous since I didn't have any family to sit with and help me. To my astonishment they asked Dan and me to be the witness couple. I was terrified. Then when we went in the room no one sat by me. The lady closest to me skipped the seat next to me. I remember feeling very alone. I remember praying for help and comfort. I then had the distinct thought and impression that my sister Julene was sitting next to me in the empty chair. A calm feeling and peace came to me, and I was able to enjoy my temple experience that day and feel Heavenly Father's love for me.

We have felt Julene's presence on at least two other times. The first time was in the Idaho Falls Temple when we completed her temple ordinances. The second time was when our youngest daughter was married. All five of our girls and their spouses were able to be in

Rexburg and attend the ceremonies in the Rexburg Temple. We felt Julene's presence on this special occasion.

We have to acknowledge that Julene not only suffered for her own refinement but also for the benefit of her family. One of my mother's favorite sayings was: "Actions speak louder than words." I think the actions of each member of our family have shown that we know the importance of being worthy to live with Julene and God once again. Our girls have each had large families and have taught their children the importance of living gospel principles—both by precept and by example. As Elder Dellenbach predicted: "The day will come that you will thank Julene for her sacrifice." That day has come!

CHAPTER FIFTEEN

JULENE SHARES HER TESTIMONY

When Julene sensed that she would not be with us for much longer, she felt like she needed to write her story. She had just received a "handy, dandy letter writing tool" from the man who was teaching her Braille from the Idaho Commission for the Blind. She first tried it out with a letter to me [as shown below], and then, with great effort, wrote her story and her testimony. It is presented without changes.

> Dear Mom, I am just writing in this to find out what it feels like and what it looks like to use this hand dandy letter writer that I got. After all, if it's a letterwriter I really should use it to write letters, right? Anyway, I just wanted to tell you how much I love you, and how glad I am that you decided to invite me into your family. I really enjoy spending my days with you - I never thought I could make such good friends with a girl - especially my mom!
>
> I also wanted to thank you for being patient with me
>
> So what do you think? Should I keep this & use it or give it to Anneli for Christmas? Just kidding.
>
> Love ya tons!,
>
> Julene

Feb 18 2000

I told Dr. Redd that I was going to stop praying for a miracle and start praying for the millennium. After considering that, I can no longer procrastinate writing my thoughts and feelings. I've had many people tell me to write a book and I would like to write a humorous narrative of some of the events that have happened since my illness occurred. But I've decided that it's more important to share my testimony. However, Nephi had 2 sets of plates . . . .

Despite all of my challenges & sorrows, I believe that I am a Child of God and that He loves me. I have had so many experiences when I have felt His love and been blessed, I have learned how much we depend on the Lord. He gives us everything. His presence and His power are exemplified in so many things. Since I lost the ability to breathe completely on my own, I have learned how limiting it is to depend on a machine and a tank of oxygen to supply each breath. I am unable to go anyplace even to the extent of being unable to move from one place in a room to another without the assistance of another person to turn up my oxygen, help me maneuver the tubings on the ventilator and sometimes to help me personally. Although I am often frustrated by my inability to do this alone, I am constantly reminded how much we each depend on the Lord for each breath we breathe, each step we take, etc.

Sunday February 20 2000 (2/20/2000)

On Wednesday my breathing was so difficult that I was having trouble wanting to keep breathing at all. Thursday, after Dr. Redd's visit, I began taking a fairly large dose of Decadron –a corticosteroid. Between that and the antibiotic I began Wednesday, I am feeling like a different person. I told my [mother] that it's kind of scary to feel so much different in such a short amount of time. The Lord has really blessed us with the developments of modern medicine. I remember when I was in the Rehab Center at Salt Lake Regional Hospital. I felt constantly frightened and longed for a sense of peace. The next day they began

112

giving me Attavan (sp?). Although a narcotic drug, I was given an immediate sense of peace and comfort—knowing that the Lord had developed these medicines to help man and man has corrupted the use of them and abused them. I know it sounds strange, but just as I believe that herbs were placed on earth for the use of man, I believe that science and modern medicine each have their place as well. I only hope that I will be able to fulfill the mission on the earth that the Lord has preserved me to do.

Several weeks ago, one of the full-time missionaries came over with another member on "splits". They shared a fictitious story about a man required to put all of his trust in the Lord. He was required to let go of everything first. I wonder whether I am willing to let go & trust that the Lord will take care of me whether modern medicine can or not. It's not easy to believe that the Lord knows better than we do, but yet I know that He is all-knowing, all-powerful, & all-present. Surely He knows better than I what I need. I am thankful for the scriptures & the comforting writings of our current General Authorities that help me put my trust in the Lord & believe that his Atonement can take away all of my suffering.

Feb 24 2000

It's been a week since my latest miracle & I don't think I will ever cease to be amazed. Tonight I ate the 2nd meal of the day (as I have for the past several days) and realized just how good it felt to be eating real food again. Although I'm sure all of the basic nutrients are provided in what we mix up, it simply doesn't feel the same. I'm so grateful not only for the opportunity to eat again, but also for the delicious and good food that we have.

I got a letter from Margo the other day telling me how much she loved me and appreciated my friendship. It made me feel rather guilty for how critical I am of her. She has been my friend for such a long time.

113

Although I am happy that she has found Dan, I miss her very much. It seems very strange that she is not coming home right away.

I also got a letter from Nick Munns today. As funny as I feel saying it, there is some special connection between us. I'm never very sure how much I want to think about it because I fear I may be quite disappointed someday, but for now having something to hope for, however small, makes all the difference in everyday life. I hope that I am as much support to him as he has been to me. I don't write often, but he always writes.

Feb 29 2000

Leap Year! Considering that this day only happens once every 4 years, I think this day should be something monumental—don't you? This morning—okay, it was afternoon by the time they got here, my Institute teacher, Mindy Davis brought her parents—Trumann G. & Ann Madsen—over to meet me. They are both very well known—writers and speakers. Brother Madsen is the speaker at Devotional today at Ricks College.

They began their visit with me by singing a cappella in 3-part harmony ~Love at Home~ It was very nice. After a few minutes of chatting, Mom asked Brother Madsen if he could offer any enlightenment on why some blessings which seem so applicable to this life are either not fulfilled, or get fulfilled "in the next life". Although there is no real answer to that question, some of the ideas that we talked about included—well the bottom line is "Do you know the Lord's will? Are your actions in accordance with His will? I think the most interesting thing about the discussion was they mentioned several examples of people whose blessings did not result [sic] in this life. Does the Lord change His mind? Of course, those are rhetorical questions, but after they left and the last thing he told Mom was, "Don't give up!" There was a beautiful feeling in the house. He said to me, "You have the face of a Saint—and I am someone who knows."

114

As he began his Devotional address, he said that he was going to set aside his prepared talk and give the thoughts from his heart and although he didn't say anything that would indicate that his visit here had altered his plans, it felt very much like his remarks were addressed to me. Perhaps that was just the Spirit working in me to gain from his talk, but it felt really cool to interpret his remarks as I felt prompted.

March 13 2000

Over the last 2 weeks I have had a number of amazing experiences. After the Madsens visited me, we decided to contact friends and family to join our ward in a special fast. Sister King from the General Relief Society Board asked if she could come up & spend the weekend with us and be part of the fast. So, she & her husband came on Saturday evening. I had just been listening to the Ensign which I get on tape because of my eyesight, and heard an article by Elder Jeffrey R. Holland called, "Cast not away thy Confidence." It talks about how adversity & trials will always be increased when we are about to or just have received special insights & blessings from the Lord. How true this article has proved for me. Saturday morning my feeding [tube] burst through the opening in my stomach wall, spilling the contents of my stomach down my front, although we were able to reinsert the tube, enough damage occurred that the balloon broke & Dr. Redd had to come to the house & insert a catheter into the track to attempt to seal it off. This happened over the Saturday night/Sunday morning when everyone was fasting for me. I couldn't understand. On Sunday, Sister King & her husband had dinner with us & President King & Dad gave me a blessing. It was a comforting blessing, one of love & the knowledge that God is in charge. Our visit was really nice. After they left, it became apparent that we would have to do something about the stomach tube before going to Salt Lake for eye surgery on Wednesday. After a few phone calls to Salt Lake—which in and of themselves were miraculous—both Dr. Bowers & Dr. Dean were on call & on hospital duty for the time we would be there. We arranged to leave for LDS hospital early Monday morning & wait until Wednesday where we would move to

Moran Eye Center & U of U hospital. Carla took Anneli and Audra down to Provo & everything fell into place.

Everything except my health. Monday morning I started coughing up blood, my feeding tube was still leaking. Dr. Dean had arranged to admit me into the Respiratory Special Care Unit at LDS for a collapsed lung/respiratory failure. So perhaps it was good for insurance purposes that I had such a scary morning! All I know is, going back to Elder Holland's article, it really seems like everything goes against you before something good happens.

But something good did happen. Tuesday night, Dr. Dean asked if he could come by and visit after his appointment in his office because he didn't have time [before]. He said he had an appointment with a church authority, ([Dr. Dean is] not LDS), Elder Hales. So after he left I went and took my first shower since leaving the Burn Unit (I have bathed, but not showered!) As I was finishing, Mom left to get some lotion. When she came back she said, "Skip the lotion. Let's get dressed. Dad is talking to Elder Hales!" So I dressed quickly and went back to my room where Elder Hales and his wife visited with us for about 20 minutes. They are both really sweet and genuinely concerned. It just made you feel good to talk to them. As he was preparing to leave, he asked if he could do anything for me. I was able to ask for a blessing. What a beautiful experience that was. It's hard for me even to describe how I felt except a great love and warmth. I tried to memorize every word and never forget them, but it's something that's hard to want to share with everyone so only parts of it stand out in my memory. This much I do know, the Lord loves me and is in charge of my future. If I can trust Him, all will be well.

EPILOGUE: TWO GIFTS

THE GIFT OF HUMOR

Even when she was very ill, Julene still had a keen sense of humor. She wanted us to remember some of the funny things that happened during this time of great stress. These are presented just as Julene wrote them:

Julene, realizing she was on oxygen, a ventilator, and a feeding system, thought the following conversation between the home health nurse and her mom was quite funny:

Nurse: "Do you have a living will for Julene?"

Mom: "Yes . . . but we're not exactly sure what to put on it—Don't put her on life support?"

Nurse to Julene: "I'm sorry—your mother has such a sick sense of humor!"

* * * * * *

Statements by Audra, my 4-year old Babysitter

- "We had a hard time putting Anneli (age 10) to bed last night, huh?"

- "I can do her eyes, but I don't know how to suction."

- "Mom's asleep, Anneli went to bed and I'm taking care of Julene all by myself."

- Audra: "Mom, I don't want to go to school when I get big."

Mom: "Oh, you just want to stay at home, and I can help you learn to read?"

Audra: "Yeah, I can stay at home and do puzzles, and I will help Julene, and maybe I can learn to suction."

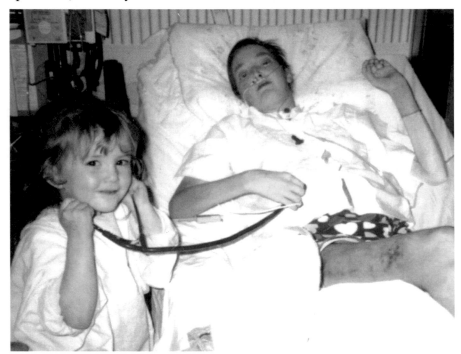

Audra pictured with Julene at the Burn Center—
(shows skin graft site on right leg)

- "I didn't miss you while I was gone, but I missed the rest of the people: Daddy & Mommy & Jessi (the dog) & the bent-cart (vent cart) and the shelf & my bunny!" . . .
- "I'm going to do it all by MYSELF—Mom, will you help me?"
- "I don't want Julene to help me!"
- "When I grow up I can be a nurse."

We were having a contest to see who could finish dinner first. When Audra saw that she might have a chance of winning she told me: "Don't take another bite, little lady."

Audra's most famous statements:

"You love me too much!"

"Can we have smashed potatoes?"

"It's in my breadroom!"

"Bless our flamily."

"I'm using my imagination,"—as she sweeps the floor.

"Can I have this can of fork & beans?"

"Where's my bi-lin (violin)?"

"Can I walk on the trettemill?"

"Jessi, Calm Down!"

"Darling—Good Night, darling."

* * * * *

Heidi, our aide, accidentally cut her finger on something. After Mom informed her that she didn't know whether we had any band-aids, she sought Audra's advice. Audra quickly led her into her bedroom where she said, "Do you want Winnie-the-Pooh or Barbie?"

* * * * *

In order to be comfortable, Julene slept with several pillows. She started replacing these pillows with some of the stuffed bears she received as gifts. She wrote this poem:

Bears
I cannot bare/bear to sleep alone
The bed feels really bare
Unless I've got one in each arm
To hold me when I'm scared

Julene was amused at how visitors tried to find tactful things to say, when they found that her condition had changed considerably:

"Your color looks great!" —Bright Red Cheeks?

After looking at my picture, saying with surprise: "Wow, You're beautiful"

* * * * *

Huge oxygen tanks were delivered about every two weeks. Julene told about one delivery man on his first trip to our house:

"We were in the process of building a shed, and there were sawhorses and lumber scraps on the driveway. Jim stepped off the back of the truck and fell onto a saw horse and ended up on the ground. Although not severely injured, it must have knocked the wind out of him because he didn't rise for several seconds.

"A few weeks later we were preparing to replace the driveway. When he delivered the tank, and he saw the preparations, he asked, 'I hope you're not doing this on account of me.' After that he introduced himself as the one who cracked the driveway until they had to replace it."

* * * * *

Julene tried to joke around about her many set-backs. She wrote this to share with some of her friends:

SOMETHING MIGHT BE WRONG IF . . .

- ❖ Getting ready for bed is down to 3-1/2 hours

- ❖ Your friends ask if you are getting over measles, and it is only your old I.V. sites

- ❖ A couple of pieces of tape on your face brings on cellulitis and 4 weeks of antibiotics

- ❖ Your doctors celebrate your "fat" legs

- ❖ The broncho-dilators cause your lungs to shut down

- ❖ Your walking distance is measured in hundredths of a mile rather than in miles

- ❖ Your idea of a dinner party is inviting the eye surgeon so he can take out the stitches in your eye

- ❖ You don't fall down the stairs to crack a rib, but rather lay in bed coughing to do so

- ❖ Your pain medication gives you a headache

- ❖ In spite of all these things, you still think you are getting better . . .

THE GIFT OF MUSIC

Two months after Julene died, our family was asked to play a 45-minute pre-show for the opening ceremonies of the Idaho International Dance Festival. When the festival committee invited us, they said they realized that Julene had recently died and would understand if we didn't feel we could present a show. We discussed this, and we decided it would be an opportunity to keep Julene's memory alive. She was the sole reason we had learned to play bluegrass music and become a family band.

With the help of our two sons-in-law, Eric and Matt, we performed for a very large crowd in front of the stadium at Ricks College (now BYU-Idaho). When we neared the end of our program, Terry dedicated our performance to the memory of Julene and her love of music.

I continued to teach a bluegrass band class at Ricks and BYU-Idaho. In total, I prepared bands to participate in ten folk-dance tours. The tours were discontinued after 2004, but the students from my classes continued to entertain each semester. We played for church dinners, campus events, and culminated each semester with a concert of our own. Students had the opportunity to provide service in the form of happy, uplifting music as well as developing their own skills and talents. Some have gone on to form their own bluegrass groups or teach members of their wards to fiddle and have fun! A couple of my former students are using their skills to teach fiddling in their school programs. At least two students have formed professional bands.

Our two youngest daughters, Anneli and Audra, both participated in my classes. When they were younger, I would sometimes use them as guests when I needed a substitute or an extra fiddler. When Anneli entered BYU-Idaho, she encouraged her friends to enroll in the bluegrass band class with her. By then she was a music major and an excellent violinist. We did some very exciting music that semester.

When Audra was in first grade, she played a piece on one of our concerts as a novelty number. This continued for about four years, while she still looked "little" but was surprisingly good. The summer she graduated from high school, we put together a band to go on tour with her clogging team. Terry played guitar, I played banjo, Audra played mandolin, our two oldest grandchildren played fiddle. We invited two young men to join us playing guitar and bass. We spent three weeks in Portugal participating in two International Dance Festivals.

As I neared retirement age, Audra begged me to keep teaching until she was old enough to actually be in the class. She participated for three semesters. The last concert I did was called, "Have a Bluegrass Christmas." We had never previously performed Christmas music bluegrass style. It was a joint concert with a group from Brigham Young University and was a great success.

Our grandchildren have all learned to play violin as soon as they were able to hold a tiny violin (or one made from a box). Many have learned other bluegrass instruments. SaraLyn and Eric's family of seven children has a bluegrass band and have performed at the Washington D. C. Temple Visitor's Center for a spring and Christmas concert, as well as performing at the Marriott Ranch for visiting dignitaries. Other families have performed at ward events and at retirement centers. Some of our grandchildren have performed in Europe with folk dance groups, as their mothers did.

We will never know how many individuals have gained valuable experiences from participation in bluegrass music. Touring with the folk-dance teams was always a spiritual experience. Entertaining is a special kind of service. This has all come about because of Julene's desire to play banjo and share her talents with others.

* * * * *

To see videos of Julene and the Wilcox family performing, and to read more about the creation of this book, you may visit:
www.oneangelandtwentyonemiracles.com

ACKNOWLEDGEMENTS

Although I tried to write about Julene's experiences at least two other times, I always put away all the notes, letters, and pictures amidst tears and emotional distress. It was such a difficult two and a half years, I was not ready to relive it!

My feelings began to change when I heard John O'Leary give a motivational talk at a convention in San Antonio in March of 2017. He told of his experiences after being burned as a 9-year old. When he told of the pain and suffering in a burn center, it brought back a flood of memories. The important thing he said was: "You all have a story; you need to share it!" I casually considered that maybe I should try writing Julene's story once again.

As we returned home the next day, Dr. Hans Redd, Julene's Rexburg doctor, was standing in a line to board the plane we had just exited. We talked for a few minutes, and he said: "In my experience as a doctor, I have never seen anyone suffer as much as Julene did." Then, two days later I received a touching letter from a man who had been deeply involved with our family situation, reminding me of the blessing of the Lord during this trying time. And again, the day after that, I just happened upon a professor Julene had been especially close to. He told me of how he visited her just a day or two before she died, and told me of their meaningful conversation. I then knew it was not only a good idea to keep her memory alive, but it was a mandate.

The task has been both arduous and rewarding. I found Julene's own brief story, written in the last few days of her life. I am not sure I had ever read that. I was reminded of the caring concern of literally hundreds of friends, workers, and even casual acquaintances. Many have written to us again and reminded us of Julene's influence in their lives. It has been an amazing journey.

My thanks to those who have given of their time and expertise. Our youngest daughter, Audra—the 4-year old nurse, had such an excellent perspective because she couldn't remember much of the trauma, but

125

only Julene's happier moments. She wasn't afraid to say: "Mom, that doesn't make any sense." At age 23, she has become a very proficient writer and a great photo editor.

Since I was trained to be a musician, not a writer, I appreciated those who helped me edit and proof-read. The novelist, Jack Weyland and his wife Sherry both said: "You need to publish this story; we will help you." Julene's voice teacher, Florence Bowman, (also a writer), said: "I would love to help you." All three have all offered such good ideas and important corrections.

It was more than coincidental that we happened to see a special friend in Provo, Utah when our granddaughter was hospitalized at Utah Valley Hospital. Our granddaughter did not experience long-term difficulties, but I benefited greatly from visiting with Janice Southern, a nurse there. We had become acquainted with her and her twin sister, Jennifer, on a Church History tour a previous summer, but I hadn't seen them for many months. I told Janice about my need for an editor to help with Julene's book, and mentioned that it would be nice if Jennifer could help. She talked to Jennifer, a secretary who works in the LDS Church Office Building, and Jennifer immediately agreed to help. She has edited many church publications and knows how to present all the scriptures and quotations from LDS sources. And best of all, I have loved working with her. We have now adopted two additional daughters.

Most of all, my husband, Terry, has read and reread the many versions of this book. We have remembered the tragic situations that took Julene from us. We also have been reminded of the many inspiring miracles that have helped us know that the Lord does watch over each one of us more closely than we realize. We are even more dedicated to becoming an "eternal family."

ABOUT THE AUTHOR

Eileen V. Wilhoit Wilcox is the mother of Julene. She received her degrees in music education and taught in the elementary schools in Rexburg. When Julene was a baby, she started teaching part-time at Ricks College and subsequently, Brigham Young University-Idaho. She is now retired but loves to say that as well as teaching piano, she taught the only class on campus that one could "fiddle around for credit— Bluegrass Band!" She and her husband, Terry, have five other daughters and one son who died when he was only a year old. They currently have twenty-three grandchildren who all do (or will) play violin!

The author welcomes your comments and questions at: oneangeland21miracles@gmail.com